Missouri Then and Now
Activity Book

Missouri Then and Now
Activity Book

Student's Edition

Pamela Fleming Lowe

University of Missouri Press
Columbia and London

Copyright © 2004 by
The Curators of the University of Missouri
University of Missouri Press, Columbia, Missouri 65201
Printed and bound in the United States of America
5 4 3   08 07

Library of Congress Cataloging-in-Publication Data

Lowe, Pamela Fleming, 1961–
  Missouri then and now activity book / Pamela Fleming Lowe.—Student's ed.
      p. cm.
  ISBN 0-8262-1540-8 (alk. paper)
  1. Missouri—Juvenile literature. 2. Missouri—History—Juvenile literature. 3. Missouri—Study and teaching
(Elementary)—Activity programs—Juvenile literature. 4. Missouri—History—Study and teaching
(Elementary)—Activity programs—Juvenile literature. I. Title.
  F466.3.L69 2004b
  977.8—dc22
                                                                        2004009864

⊗™ This paper meets the requirements of the
American National Standard for Permanence of Paper
for Printed Library Materials, Z39.48, 1984.

Designer: Pamela Fleming Lowe
Printer and binder: Thomson-Shore, Inc.
Typeface: Agency FB

Contents

Letter to Students   vii
Missouri History Trading Cards   ix

Chapter 1   The First Missourians   1
Chapter 2   A Rich Land   13
Chapter 3   Europe Discovers America and Missouri   25
Chapter 4   Life in French Missouri   37
Chapter 5   Missouri Becomes a Part of the United States   51
Chapter 6   Life on the Frontier   65
Chapter 7   Early Travel   77
Chapter 8   Missouri and the West   89
Chapter 9   A Growing State   101
Chapter 10   A Divided Country   115
Chapter 11   The Civil War Comes to Missouri   131
Chapter 12   Reconstruction in Missouri   145
Chapter 13   Changing Times in Missouri   157
Chapter 14   Some Good Times and Bad Times   173
Chapter 15   Missourians Join Struggles in Faraway Places and at Home   185
Chapter 16   Government in Missouri   197
Chapter 17   Missouri at the Start of the Twenty-first Century   213
Chapter 18   Fine Arts in Missouri   225

Web Site Bibliography   239

Dear Students,

This activity book was created to accompany the *Missouri Then and Now* textbook in order to assist you in learning more about Missouri's rich history. These stimulating activities will help you to learn how the state of Missouri came into existence and how it has touched not only the lives of the many people that have lived here, but also the history of our entire country. You will discover where early Missourians came from, how Missouri became the state we know and love, and where your generation of Missourians is headed. Learning about Missouri's history will help you make discoveries about yourself as well.

As you complete each chapter of the *"Missouri Then and Now" Activity Book,* I would like you to consider this: Your period in Missouri history is certainly different from that of the early Missouri people, but one thing that has remained the same is that actions have consequences. Whether a decision is good or bad, it has consequences. You will learn how decisions made by early Missourians affected other choices and ultimately affected history. The early people of Missouri probably gave little thought to the history they were making—but here we are centuries later, reading about their lives and adventures. What happens in Missouri in your lifetime will also be recorded for future generations. For you are Missourians and the historians of your generation. You will help to lead Missouri into the future. Whatever you choose to become or achieve will make an impact on our state and on yourself. Remember to take pride in being from Missouri. It will always be a part of you and your history.

Sincerely,
Pamela Fleming Lowe

MISSOURI HISTORY TRADING CARDS

Create trading cards about important figures from a chapter that will be chosen by your teacher. Write the figures' names and draw their pictures on the front of the cards. Write down information about each person on the back of the cards.

MISSOURI HISTORY TRADING CARDS (cont.)

Complete your Missouri history trading cards by writing important information about each person on the back of the cards. Include vital information such as the person's birthplace and years of birth and death as well as the person's contribution to Missouri history.

Missouri Then and Now
Activity Book

CHAPTER 1: THE FIRST MISSOURIANS

OBJECTIVES

Spaces are provided below each objective for notes taken during reading and class discussions of the chapter and to assist in preparation for the chapter assessment.

In Chapter 1, we will discover and learn about:

The First Missourians

Archaeologists

Missouri's First Farmers

The Influence of the European Explorers

1

OBJECTIVES (continued)

The Origin of Missouri's Name

The Legacy of the Native Americans and How They Came to America

The Various Native American Tribes of Missouri

Contributions of the Osage Women to Their Tribe

Name: _____

VOCABULARY INSIGHTS

1. archaeologist

    a. Definition: _____

    _____

    b. Write a sentence from the chapter using the word: _____

    _____

    c. Create your own sentence: _____

    _____

    d. Illustrate the word:

2. bison

    a. Definition: _____

    _____

    b. Write a sentence from the chapter using the word: _____

    _____

    c. Create your own sentence: _____

    _____

    d. Illustrate the word:

VOCABULARY INSIGHTS (cont.)

3. bog

    a. Definition: _____

_____

    b. Write a sentence from the chapter using the word: _____

_____

    c. Create your own sentence: _____

_____

    d. Illustrate the word:

4. game

    a. Definition: _____

_____

    b. Write a sentence from the chapter using the word: _____

_____

    c. Create your own sentence: _____

_____

    d. Illustrate the word:

Name: _____

THE EUROPEAN INFLUENCE

The European influx into Missouri changed the lives of Native Americans. The Europeans brought with them many new things that they traded. These items made the lives of the Native Americans much easier.

Using inference skills, describe how trade with the Europeans influenced Native Americans' clothing, meals, travel, and hunting practices.

Clothing	_____ _____ _____
Meals	_____ _____ _____
Travel	_____ _____ _____
Hunting Practices	_____ _____ _____

Name: _____

TIMELINE

Choose five events from Chapter 1 in your textbook and create a timeline. Write an appropriate title for your timeline in the box provided.

6

Name: _____

IDENTIFYING GROUPS

List five groups of First Missourians, using Chapter 1 in your textbook. Add some details about them in the spaces provided, using complete sentences.

1. [_____]

_____

_____

_____

_____

2. [_____]

_____

_____

_____

_____

3. [_____]

_____

_____

_____

_____

4. [_____]

_____

_____

_____

_____

5. [_____]

_____

_____

_____

_____

Name: _____

CAUSE AND EFFECT

The Europeans brought trade to Missouri. Trade and the use of guns changed the Native Americans' lives and environment. Fill in the cause-and-effect chart detailing the effects on the Native Americans.

THE CAUSE

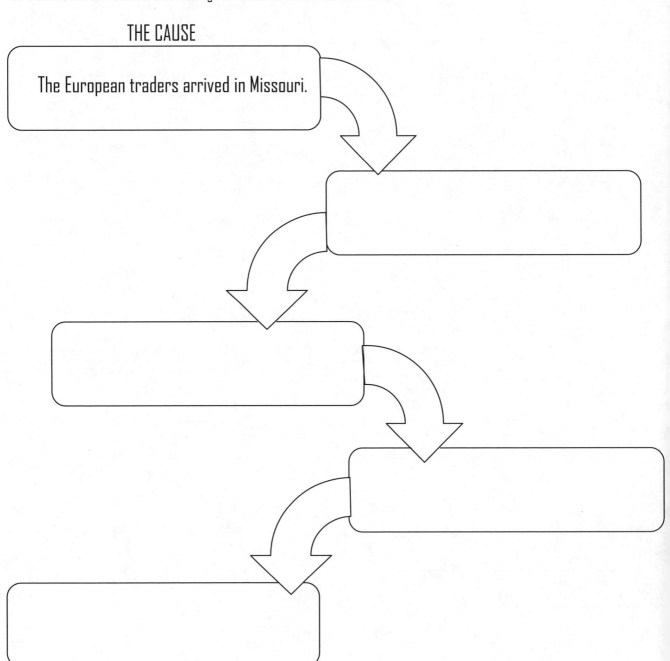

The European traders arrived in Missouri.

Name: _____

CHAPTER 1 ASSESSMENT

Short Answers

1. Who were the first Missourians? _____

2. What type of scientists dig up the ground where early people once lived and look for things that they made?

    _____

3. Who were Missouri's first real farmers? _____

4. What was the worst problem the Indians faced when the Europeans arrived?

    _____

5. Explain how Missouri got its name. _____

    _____

6. Explain in your own words what the Native Americans have given us. _____

    _____

    _____

7. How do archaeologists learn about people who lived long ago? _____

    _____

    _____

8. How do some scientists speculate that Native Americans came to America?

    _____

    _____

9. What valuable lesson do you think Native Americans learned too late about hunting animals?

    _____

    _____

(continued on next page)

9

Name: _____

CHAPTER 1 ASSESSMENT (cont.)

Demonstrating Your Knowledge

10. Write a short paragraph explaining the positive and negative influences the Europeans had on the Native American way of life.

11. Write a short paragraph explaining the importance of the Osage women to their tribe.

(continued on next page)

Name: _____

CHAPTER 1 ASSESSMENT (cont.)

12. Compare and contrast two Missouri tribes of your choice using a diagram. Include three facts about each tribe and three ways in which the tribes are different. Create a title for your diagram.

(continued on next page)

Name: _____

CHAPTER 1 ASSESSMENT (cont.)

Vocabulary

13. Below is a word used in the chapter. In the spaces provided, write a definition of the word, list a synonym for the word, and draw a picture that illustrates the word's meaning.

archaeologist

Definition

Synonym

Illustrate the word

14. Explain how the word relates to the chapter. _____

_____

CHAPTER 2: A RICH LAND

OBJECTIVES

Spaces are provided below each objective for notes taken during reading and class discussions of the chapter and to assist in preparation for the chapter assessment.

In Chapter 2, we will discover and learn about:

The Seven Continents

Missouri's Neighboring States

Ozark Highland

Southeast Lowland

OBJECTIVES (cont.)

Western Plain

Northern Plain

Native Americans: The First Settlers in Missouri

Missouri Rivers

Name: _____

VOCABULARY INSIGHTS

1. continent

    a. Definition: _____

_____

    b. Write a sentence from the chapter using the word: _____

_____

    c. Create your own sentence: _____

_____

    d. Illustrate the word:

2. electricity

    a. Definition: _____

_____

    b. Write a sentence from the chapter using the word: _____

_____

    c. Create your own sentence: _____

_____

    d. Illustrate the word:

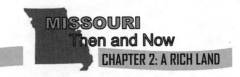

VOCABULARY INSIGHTS (cont.)

3. spring

    a. Definition: _____

    _____

    b. Write a sentence from the chapter using the word: _____

    _____

    c. Create your own sentence: _____

    _____

    d. Illustrate the word:

4. soybeans

    a. Definition: _____

    _____

    b. Write a sentence from the chapter using the word: _____

    _____

    c. Create your own sentence: _____

    _____

    d. Illustrate the word:

Name: _____

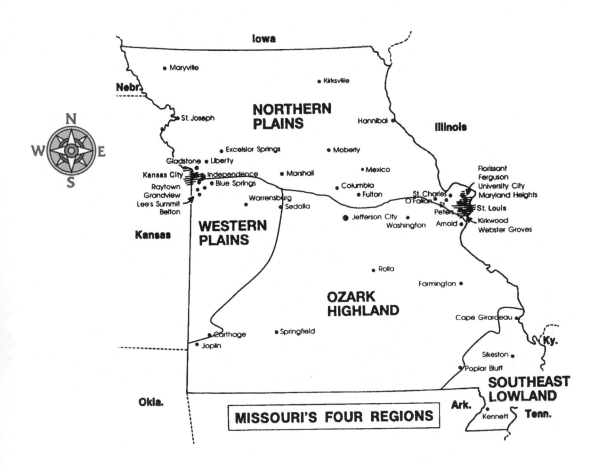

1. Which state is directly south of Missouri? _____

2. Which region contains Blue Springs? _____

3. Starting in Hannibal and traveling south to Rolla, which regions would you pass through?

   _____

4. Which region is the smallest? _____

5. In which region is the city of Liberty? _____

6. According to the map, how many regions are in Missouri? _____

Name: _____

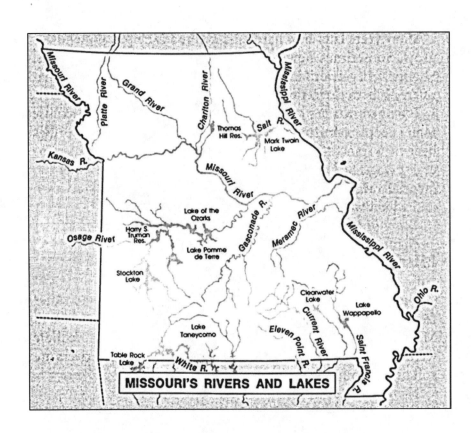

MISSOURI'S RIVERS AND LAKES

1. The Missouri and Mississippi Rivers join near St. Louis. Put a star on the map where the two rivers join.

2. The Mississippi River forms the eastern border of the state of Missouri and flows from the _____ to the _____, down to the Gulf of Mexico.

3. After it flows south down the northwest border of Missouri, the Missouri River generally flows from _____ to _____ across the state.

4. The largest lake in the state is the Lake of the Ozarks. If you were to travel west, what river would take you into the state of Kansas? _____

5. *Using critical thinking:* List two reasons the chosen location for St. Louis was near two major rivers.

    a. _____

    b. _____

Maryville

Kirksville

Hannibal

Excelsior Springs

Moberly

St.

Gladstone • Liberty

Kansas City • Independence • Marshall

Mexico

Raytown • Blue Springs

Columbia

Florissant
Ferguson
University City
Maryland Heights

Grandview

Warrensburg

Fulton

St. Charles
O'Fallon

St.
Peters

St. Louis

Lee's Summit

Sedalia

Belt

Jefferson City

Washington

Arnold

Kirkwood
Webster Groves

Rolla

Farmington •

Cape Girardeau

Carthage

S

Sikeston •

Joplin

Popl

MISSOURI'S FOUR REGIONS

Kennett

1. Label the eight states bordering Missouri.

2. Label the four regions of Missouri.

3. Draw and label the Missouri and Mississippi Rivers.

Name: _____

TAUM SAUK MOUNTAIN SCAVENGER HUNT

Go to the Taum Sauk Mountain State Park web site to find the answers to the following questions.

http://www.mostateparks.com/taumsauk/geninfo.htm

1. How was Taum Sauk Mountain formed? _____

   _____

2. How tall is the mountain at its peak, which is the highest point in Missouri? _____

3. How many acres are in the surrounding park? _____

4. In which Missouri region does the mountain reside? _____

5. What is the name for the rocky openings in which you can see the park's volcanic origin? _____

6. What two valuable services do the natural communities of Taum Sauk provide?

   a. _____

   _____

   b. _____

   _____

7. What is the name of the state's tallest waterfall? _____

8. What do the land managers do to help preserve the open woodlands? _____

9. What is the Devil's Tollgate? _____

Name: _____

CHAPTER 2 ASSESSMENT

Vocabulary

1. Below is a word used in the chapter. In the spaces provided, write a definition of the word, list a synonym for the word, and draw a picture that illustrates the word's meaning.

continent

Definition

Synonym

Illustrate the word

2. Explain how the word relates to the chapter. _____

_____

(continued on next page)

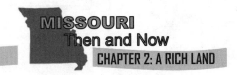
Name: _____

CHAPTER 2 ASSESSMENT (cont.)

Short Answers

3. Name the seven continents: _____, _____, _____,

    _____, _____, _____, _____

4. On which continent is Missouri located? _____

5. What country is north of the United States? _____

6. What country is south of the United States? _____

7. List the eight states that border Missouri: _____, _____, _____,

    _____, _____, _____, _____, _____

8. Name Missouri's two most important rivers: _____, _____

9. What is the highest point in the state? _____

10. What is Missouri's largest lake? _____

11. What type of climate does Missouri have? _____

True or False

12. _____   Missouri is located on the continent of South America.

13. _____   Canada is located north of the United States.

14. _____   Mt. Everest is the highest point in Missouri.

15. _____   The largest lake in Missouri is the Lake of the Ozarks.

16. _____   The Missouri River and the Mississippi River are Missouri's most important rivers.

17. _____   Missouri has a polar climate.

18. _____   The Ozark Highlands is the best region for growing crops.

19. _____   Iowa is south of Missouri.

20. _____   The Northern Plains has fewer mineral resources than other parts of the state.

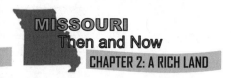
CHAPTER 2 ASSESSMENT (cont.)

Short Answers

21. Why is Missouri sometimes called the "heart of America"? _____

_____

22. Why did fewer people settle in the Ozarks region of Missouri? _____

_____

23. Why did so many different Indian peoples decide to live in Missouri? _____

_____

Demonstrating Your Knowledge

24. Give reasons why early settlers would settle in each of the four Missouri regions.

Southeast Lowland:

Ozark Highlands:

Western Plains:

Northern Plains:

Name: _____

CHAPTER 2 ASSESSMENT (cont.)

25. The environment and way of life in Missouri has changed in many ways since the Native Americans discovered that it was a rich land. Write a paragraph and create an illustration to compare and contrast the Missouri of long ago and the Missouri of today.

MISSOURI
Then and Now
CHAPTER 3: EUROPE DISCOVERS AMERICA & MISSOURI

OBJECTIVES

Spaces are provided below each objective for notes taken during reading and class discussions of the chapter and to assist in preparation for the chapter assessment.

In Chapter 3, we will discover and learn about:

European Explorers

Da Gama:

Columbus:

De Soto:

Marquette and Jolliet:

La Salle:

OBJECTIVES (cont.)

Ste. Genevieve Settlement

The Founding of St. Louis

The Importance of Salt

Fort Orleans

VOCABULARY INSIGHTS

1. canoe

a. Definition: _____

_____

b. Write a sentence from the chapter using the word: _____

_____

c. Create your own sentence: _____

_____

d. Illustrate the word:

2. island

a. Definition: _____

_____

b. Write a sentence from the chapter using the word: _____

_____

c. Create your own sentence: _____

_____

d. Illustrate the word:

CHAPTER 3: EUROPE DISCOVERS AMERICA & MISSOURI

VOCABULARY INSIGHTS (cont.)

3. kettle

    a. Definition: _____

    _____

    b. Write a sentence from the chapter using the word: _____

    _____

    c. Create your own sentence: _____

    _____

    d. Illustrate the word:

4. perfumes

    a. Definition: _____

    _____

    b. Write a sentence from the chapter using the word: _____

    _____

    c. Create your own sentence: _____

    _____

    d. Illustrate the word:

Name: _____

CHAPTER 3: EUROPE DISCOVERS AMERICA & MISSOURI

EUROPEAN EXPLORERS

Use the graphic organizer below to list the goals, accomplishments, and other information about the following European explorers.

Da Gama	Columbus	Marquette and Jolliet	La Salle

29

Name: _____

THE IMPORTANCE OF SALT

Write a paragraph from a young French settler's viewpoint describing the importance of salt in the lives of settlers in Missouri. For additional information, visit http://www.mostateparks.com/booneslick/geninfo.htm

Name: _____

PLANNING A CITY: Part A

Using your knowledge of the founding of St. Louis and the necessities required for people to survive, write a paragraph describing how you would plan a city in early Missouri.

Be sure to include each of the following:
- the type of soil or region
- important geographic or landscape features
- your future plans for your city
- the name of the city
- the reason for that name

You may wish to use the maps on pages 31 and 38 in the textbook as a reference.

Online resources:
- The founding of St. Louis:
  http://www.nps.gov/jeff/LewisClark2/Circa1804/StLouis/BlockInfo/Block7Efounding.htm
- St. Louis history: http://www.nps.gov/jeff/1more1.htm#Top

PLANNING A CITY: Part B

Draw a diagram of the plans you wrote about on the **Planning a City: Part A** page. Be sure to include the details you listed as important: landscape features, region, name of city, etc.

Name: _____

CHAPTER 3 ASSESSMENT

Short Answers

1. What were Columbus and Da Gama looking for? _____

2. Who were the first settlers in Ste. Genevieve? _____

3. St. Louis became the center of the _____ .

4. Who were the first Europeans to explore in Missouri? _____

   _____

5. What did the locations of Ste. Genevieve and St. Louis have in common? _____

   _____

6. Why did the French decide to settle in Missouri? _____

   _____

   _____

7. Give three reasons why salt was important to the early settlers.

   a. _____

   b. _____

   c. _____

8. Who was the first European explorer to discover the Mississippi River? _____

9. How did Spain get rich from exploring the Americas? _____

   _____

(continued on next page)

Name: _____

CHAPTER 3 ASSESSMENT (cont.)

Vocabulary

10. Below is a word used in the chapter. In the spaces provided, write a definition of the word, list a synonym for the word, and draw a picture that illustrates the word's meaning.

island

Definition

Synonym

Illustrate the word

11. Explain how the word relates to the chapter. _____

_____

Name: _____

CHAPTER 3 ASSESSMENT (cont.)

True or False

12. _____ Missouri was part of Louisiana.

13. _____ The oldest city in Missouri is Ste. Genevieve.

14. _____ Pierre Laclede was a Spanish merchant.

15. _____ The first settlers in Ste. Genevieve were French farmers and African slaves.

16. _____ Portugal was one of the first European nations to look for a better way to get to Asia.

17. _____ Amerigo Vespucci discovered the Mississippi River near where Memphis, Tennessee, stands today.

Demonstrating Your Knowledge

18. How was the location of St. Louis vital to its becoming an important settlement? Explain your answer.

19. Explain why Fort Orleans was not successful.

(continued on next page)

Name: _____

CHAPTER 3 ASSESSMENT (cont.)

Demonstrating Your Knowledge

20. Write a paragraph about a person from the chapter that you feel made the biggest contribution to Missouri. Explain your reasoning.

OBJECTIVES

Spaces are provided below each objective for notes taken during reading and class discussions of the chapter and to assist in preparation for the chapter assessment.

In Chapter 4, we will discover and learn about:

French Houses

African Americans in French Communities

Indian Neighbors

Farming

OBJECTIVES (cont.)

French Women

French Customs

Fur Trading/Lead Mining

Jeanette Fourchet

38

Name: _____

VOCABULARY INSIGHTS

1. chandelier

    a. Definition: _____

    _____

    b. Write a sentence from the chapter using the word: _____

    _____

    c. Create your own sentence: _____

    _____

    d. Illustrate the word:

2. cupboard

    a. Definition: _____

    _____

    b. Write a sentence from the chapter using the word: _____

    _____

    c. Create your own sentence: _____

    _____

    d. Illustrate the word:

VOCABULARY INSIGHTS (cont.)

3. moccasin

    a. Definition: _____

_____

    b. Write a sentence from the chapter using the word: _____

_____

    c. Create your own sentence: _____

_____

    d. Illustrate the word:

4. mortar and pestle

    a. Definition: _____

_____

    b. Write a sentence from the chapter using the words: _____

_____

    c. Create your own sentence: _____

_____

    d. Illustrate the words:

Name: _____

FRENCH CUSTOMS

Demonstrate your knowledge of the French settlers that came to Missouri in each category below. Include details about the French and how they lived in their villages.

Cooking	Schools	Entertainment	Clothing

Name: _____

AFRICAN AMERICANS AND NATIVE AMERICANS

Compare and contrast the roles of African Americans and Native Americans in the early French communities.

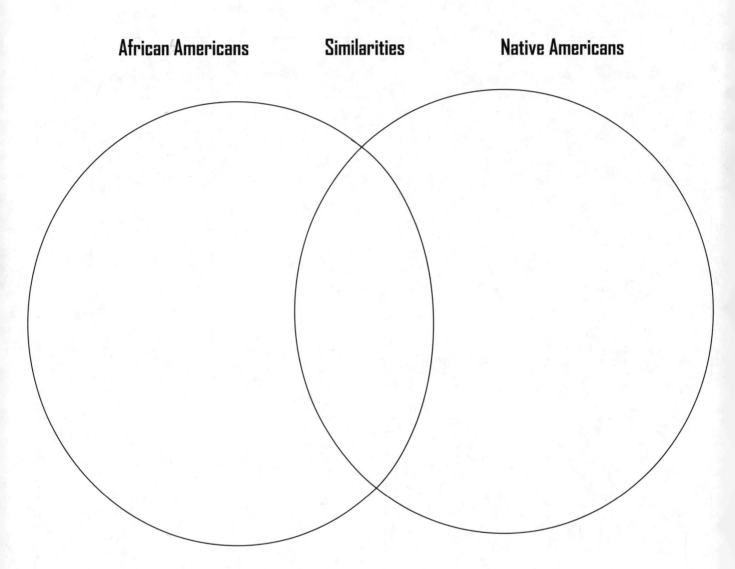

African Americans   **Similarities**   **Native Americans**

Name: _____

ARCHITECTURAL INVENTIVENESS: Part A

The French settlers were very resourceful people. They used their creativity to build homes that would accommodate their living conditions and surroundings. Choose one of the four Missouri regions. Using your own creativity, write a paragraph describing the features you would include in a home to accommodate the landscape distinctiveness of that region.

Name: _____

ARCHITECTURAL INVENTIVENESS: Part B

Draw a picture of the house you described, portraying the features you included.

Name: _____

FRENCH HOMES VS. AMERICAN LOG HOMES

Create an American log cabin or a French home. Be creative in designing the structures while maintaining cultural accuracy. One suggestion for making a home is to use an empty milk carton or juice container. One way to make logs is to wrap newspaper or construction paper around a pencil or straw. Other materials you could use are paint, cardboard, and craft sticks.

You may use your book or any other reference material for assistance, including the links below:

- Ste. Genevieve French Homes: http://www.saintegenevievetourism.org/homes.htm

- Nathan Boone Homestead: http://www.mostateparks.com/boonehome/photos.htm

Name: _____

CHAPTER 4 ASSESSMENT

True or False

1. ____ The French built their houses close together.

2. ____ All children in French Missouri went to school.

3. ____ François Valle II was a black slave.

4. ____ A French log house was different from an American log cabin.

5. ____ The French got along well with the Native Americans.

6. ____ The first European settlers in Missouri were Spanish.

7. ____ The food called gumbo came from Africa.

8. ____ Most French settlers lived in stone homes.

9. ____ A *chandelier* is a club-shaped tool used for grinding or pounding something into a powder.

10. ____ The French were a fun-loving people.

Short Answers

11. What did the French call the porches around their homes? _____

12. Louis Lorimier founded the town of _____.

13. What city became an important place for selling furs? _____

14. French lead mining was important around what city? _____

15. What is a "common field"? _____

_____

16. How were French houses different from American log cabins? _____

_____

17. Why were African Americans so important in French Missouri? _____

_____

Name: _____

CHAPTER 4 ASSESSMENT (cont.)

Demonstrating Your Knowledge

18. Explain how French villages in Missouri were different from American towns.

19. Write a paragraph explaining the role of French women in Missouri.

(continued on next page)

Name: _____

CHAPTER 4 ASSESSMENT (cont.)

20. If you were to travel back in time to live in French Missouri, would you rather be a French settler, an African American, a Native American, or a French woman? Explain your choice.

(continued on next page)

Name: _____

CHAPTER 4 ASSESSMENT (cont.)

Vocabulary

21. Below is a phrase used in the chapter, In the spaces provided, write a definition of the these words, list a synonym, and draw a picture that illustrates the words' meaning.

mortar and pestle

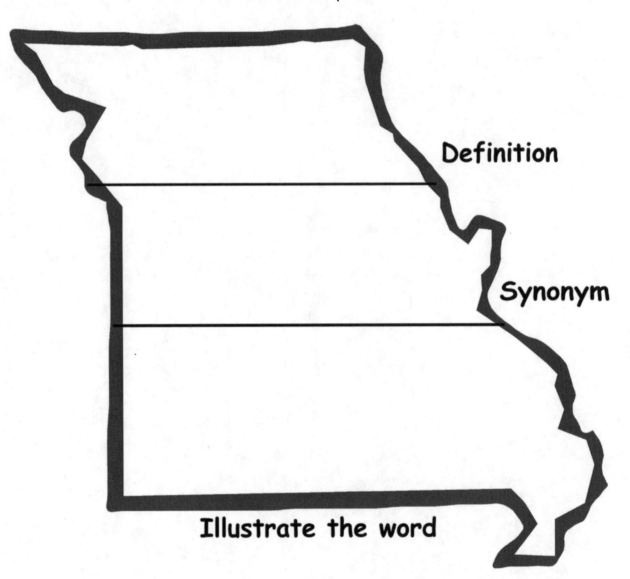

Definition

Synonym

Illustrate the word

22. Explain how the words relate to the chapter. _____

_____

50

OBJECTIVES

Spaces are provided below each objective for notes taken during reading and class discussions of the chapter and to assist in preparation for the chapter assessment.

In Chapter 5, we will discover and learn about:

The American Revolution

Daniel Boone

The Louisiana Purchase

Statehood

OBJECTIVES (cont.)

The Missouri Constitution

St. Charles and Jefferson City

Lewis and Clark

The Missouri Compromise

52

MISSOURI
Then and Now

Name: _____

CHAPTER 5: MISSOURI BECOMES A PART OF THE UNITED STATES

VOCABULARY INSIGHTS

1. botanist

a. Definition: _____

_____

b. Write a sentence from the chapter using the word: _____

_____

c. Create your own sentence: _____

_____

d. Illustrate the word:

2. boatmen

a. Definition: _____

_____

b. Write a sentence from the chapter using the word: _____

_____

c. Create your own sentence: _____

_____

d. Illustrate the word:

53

CHAPTER 5: MISSOURI BECOMES A PART OF THE UNITED STATES

VOCABULARY INSIGHTS (cont.)

3. flatboat

    a. Definition: _____

_____

    b. Write a sentence from the chapter using the word: _____

_____

    c. Create your own sentence: _____

_____

    d. Illustrate the word:

4. venison

    a. Definition: _____

_____

    b. Write a sentence from the chapter using the word: _____

_____

    c. Create your own sentence: _____

_____

    d. Illustrate the word:

54

Name: _____

THE LOUISIANA PURCHASE

The United States In 1803

Owned By England

Oregon Country

Ohio River

Pacific Ocean

Owned By Spain

Atlantic Ocean

Gulf Of Mexico

1. Draw the Mississippi River in red.

2. Label the Louisiana Purchase tract of land.

3. Label the original United States prior to the purchase of the Louisiana Territory.

4. After the purchase of the Louisiana territory, what happened to the size of the United States? _____

5. What natural landform created the border between the old United States and the new Louisiana Territory?

   _____

6. What ruler sold the Louisiana Territory to the United States? _____

7. What did the United States pay for the Louisiana Purchase? _____

8. Draw the state of Missouri in black in its approximate location on the map.

9. The Louisiana Purchase was an important event for Missourians because _____.

10. If the United States had never bought the Louisiana Territory, what country would you probably live in today?

    _____

THE LOUISIANA PURCHASE AND MISSOURI

The year is 1803 and you are writing from your home in Missouri to your cousin in Kentucky to tell him/her the news of your American citizenship. Explain in your letter how this exciting event happened.

Name: _____

MISSOURI COMPROMISE

Use the Word Bank below to fill in the blanks in the following paragraph about the Missouri Compromise. (Hint: Read the paragraph through one time before filling in the blanks and check to make sure that your sentences make sense.)

Missourians knew that citizens of a _____ had more freedom to _____ themselves

than citizens of a _____, so they asked the United States Congress to make Missouri a state.

Each state had to decide if its people could own _____. Missourians wanted their state to be a

_____ state. At the time, there were already eleven slave states and eleven free states. Many

northerners did not want any more slave states. The disagreement over _____ kept Missouri

out of the Union for more than two years. As with any disagreement that needs to be resolved, a

_____ was made. Missouri entered the _____ as a slave state. And Maine, which wanted

to become a state as well, agreed to enter the Union as a _____ state. Congress agreed to

keep slavery out of all the _____ parts of the Louisiana Territory except Missouri.

The agreement was called the Missouri Compromise.

Word Bank: state   slave   territory   slavery   compromise

free   slaves   Union   govern   northern

57

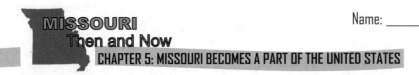
CONSTITUTIONS

Our textbook defines *constitution* as the basic law or rules of government for a nation, state, or organized group. We have learned that Missourians had to write a constitution for their new state in 1820. You can find the Missouri Constitution online at http://www.moga.state.mo.us/const/moconstn.htm. In Chapter 16, we will be learning more about our state's constitution.

In this activity, the class will divide into groups to create a classroom constitution. Use your basic knowledge of the word *constitution* and your experience as a student to help write a constitution that will explain the type of classroom government and atmosphere you would like to have. (Hint: Brainstorm with others and discuss rules that would and wouldn't work well in your classroom. Discuss what makes a good learning environment.)

Our Class Constitution

Bill of Rights

A bill of rights protects people's rights. What type of rights would you want protected in the classroom? List five below.

1.

2.

3.

4.

5.

Basic Constitution

Explain the type of classroom atmosphere you think would be beneficial to students in your class.

Name: _____

CHAPTER 5 ASSESSMENT

Vocabulary

1. Below is a word used in the chapter. In the spaces provided, write a definition of the word, list a synonym for the word, and draw a picture that illustrates the word's meaning.

botanist

Definition

Synonym

Illustrate the word

2. Explain how the word relates to the chapter. _____

_____

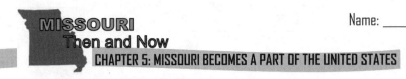

Name: _____

CHAPTER 5 ASSESSMENT (cont.)

Short Answers

3. Who wrote the Declaration of Independence and was president at the time of the Louisiana Purchase?

    _____

4. Who was the first president of the United States? _____

5. Who was the first governor of Missouri? _____

6. What two famous explorers were sent by Thomas Jefferson to explore the Missouri River to the northwest?

    _____ and _____

7. From what states did most of Missouri's settlers come? _____,

    _____, _____, and _____

8. What three countries owned early Missouri? _____, _____, and _____

9. Missouri became a state in the year _____.

10. Missouri's new constitution said that the state capital should be located on what river near the center of the state?

    _____

11. Name the agreement that stated that Missouri would enter the Union as a slave state and Maine as a free state while keeping slavery out of all the northern parts of the Louisiana Territory except Missouri.

    _____

(continued on next page)

Name: _____

CHAPTER 5 ASSESSMENT (cont.)

True or False
If a statement is false, write the correction on the blank to the right of the statement. (This applies only to statements marked false.)

12. _____ Missourians moved the capital from Hannibal to Jefferson City. _____

13. _____ The Louisiana Purchase occurred in 1903. _____

14. _____ Daniel Boone spent his last years living in Missouri. _____

15. _____ Thomas Jefferson wrote the Declaration of Independence in 1776. _____

16. _____ Fort Osage was a United States military post overlooking the Missouri River. _____

17. _____ Southern states were slave states during the Civil War. _____

18. _____ Missouri entered the Union as a free state. _____

19. _____ Missouri's first constitution allowed only men to vote. _____

20. _____ The United States bought the Louisiana Territory from Spain. _____

continued on next page)

Name: _____

CHAPTER 5 ASSESSMENT (cont.)

Demonstrating Your Knowledge

21. Write in fairy-tale form the story of how Missouri became a part of the United States. Begin your story with Spain making an offer to settlers and Daniel Boone to come live in Missouri, and end with the Missouri Compromise and Missouri becoming a state.

Once upon a time . . .

(continued on next page)

Name: _____

CHAPTER 5 ASSESSMENT (cont.)

Timeline

22. Put the following events in the order that they occurred in history.

Missouri becomes a state	Louisiana is returned to France
France gives Louisiana to Spain	Missouri state capitol moved to Jefferson City
Daniel Boone moves to Missouri	Lewis and Clark depart to explore the Northwest
United States purchases Louisiana	Declaration of Independence is written

A. _____

B. _____

C. _____

D. _____

E. _____

F. _____

G. _____

H. _____

OBJECTIVES

Spaces are provided below each objective for notes taken during reading and class discussions of the chapter and to assist in preparation for the chapter assessment.

In Chapter 6, we will discover and learn about:

Pioneer Farmers

Pioneer Women Roles

Pioneer Schools and Churches

The Ozarks

CHAPTER 6: LIFE ON THE FRONTIER

OBJECTIVES (cont.)

Nathan Boone

Cabins

Pioneer Doctors

The Cooperative Spirit of the Pioneers

66

Name: _____

VOCABULARY INSIGHTS

1. almanac

    a. Definition: _____

_____

    b. Write a sentence from the chapter using the word: _____

_____

    c. Create your own sentence: _____

_____

    d. Illustrate the word:

2. democracy

    a. Definition: _____

_____

    b. Write a sentence from the chapter using the word: _____

_____

    c. Create your own sentence: _____

_____

    d. Illustrate the word:

VOCABULARY INSIGHTS (cont.)

3. ferry

a. Definition: _____

_____

b. Write a sentence from the chapter using the word: _____

_____

c. Create your own sentence: _____

_____

d. Illustrate the word:

4. remedy

a. Definition: _____

_____

b. Write a sentence from the chapter using the word: _____

_____

c. Create your own sentence: _____

_____

d. Illustrate the word:

Name: _____

NATHAN BOONE SCAVENGER HUNT

Search the following web site to answer questions about the life of Nathan Boone.

http://www.mostateparks.com/boonehome/geninfo.htm

1. Nathan had more than one career in his lifetime. For what was he best known? _____

2. What business did he open with his brother, Daniel Morgan? _____

3. According to the Historic Site Map, in which region of Missouri is the family home of Nathan Boone located?

    _____

4. What was Nathan Boone's approximate age at the end of his life? _____

5. Nathan's home was built with a covered breezeway in the middle. According to the textbook, why did the pioneers build these dogtrots in their cabins? _____

6. Who besides family members were buried on the property? _____

7. Create a timeline of Nathan's life.

Name: _____

GRAPHIC ORGANIZER

Compare the past with the present by listing facts for the following four categories.

	Pioneer Times	The Present	
Schools			Describe the Similarities in Schooling
Homes			Describe the Similarities in Homes
Church			Describe the Similarities in Church Activities
Fun Activities			Describe the Similarities in Entertainment

Name: _____

COMPARING THE PAST WITH THE PRESENT

Use the information gathered on your graphic organizer to write about the similarities and differences between pioneer times and today. Make a rough draft on notebook paper and write your final version on this workbook page.

Name: _____

DEMOCRACY: A CLASS DISCUSSION

According to the Cambridge dictionary, democracy is the belief in freedom and equality between people, or a system of government based on this belief, in which power is held either by elected representatives or directly by the people themselves.

A democratic country and government is what Thomas Jefferson had in mind for the United States when he became president, as noted in his first inaugural address. Here is an excerpt from this address:

> During the contest of opinion through which we have passed the animation of discussions and of exertions has sometimes worn an aspect which might impose on strangers unused to think freely and to speak and to write what they think; but this being now decided by the voice of the nation, announced according to the rules of the Constitution, all will, of course, arrange themselves under the will of the law, and unite in common efforts for the common good. All, too, will bear in mind this sacred principle, that though the will of the majority is in all cases to prevail, that will to be rightful must be reasonable; that the minority possess their equal rights, which equal law must protect, and to violate would be oppression. Let us, then, fellow-citizens, unite with one heart and one mind. Let us restore to social intercourse that harmony and affection without which liberty and even life itself are but dreary things. And let us reflect that, having banished from our land that religious intolerance under which mankind so long bled and suffered, we have yet gained little if we countenance a political intolerance as despotic, as wicked, and capable of as bitter and bloody persecutions.

(To read Jefferson's first inaugural address in its entirety, go to http://www.bartleby.com/124/pres16.html)

After discussing democracy, its definition, Jefferson's dream of democracy in his inaugural address, and the knowledge that a democratic society encourages people to think, speak, and write freely, answer the following questions in paragraph form.

Why did American pioneers believe schools were important? What role did schools play in shaping citizens? Is this still true today? Why would a democratic society benefit from educated people?

Name: _____

CHAPTER 6 ASSESSMENT

Short Answers

1. Why did many settlers want to settle in Missouri in the early 1800s? _____

    _____

2. What did pioneers look for when looking for land? _____

    _____

3. After building a cabin, what was the next thing that pioneers set out to do? _____

    _____

4. In what ways were the Indians' and pioneers' lives similar? _____

    _____

5. With so few doctors on the frontier, who were the caregivers when people were sick? _____

    _____

6. The pioneers who settled in the Ozarks came mostly from the hill country of _____ and

    _____.

7. Why did the pioneers prefer to plant corn? _____

    _____

8. What did pioneers do for fun? _____

    _____

9. The most important place in a pioneer's log cabin was the _____.

10. The covered breezeway between two rooms of a cabin was called a _____.

11. A country run by the people is called a _____.

12. Traveling ministers were also called _____.

13. Large outdoor religious meetings were called _____.

Name: _____

CHAPTER 6 ASSESSMENT (cont.)

Vocabulary

14. Below is a word used in the chapter. In the spaces provided, write a definition of the word, list a synonym for the word, and draw a picture that illustrates the word's meaning.

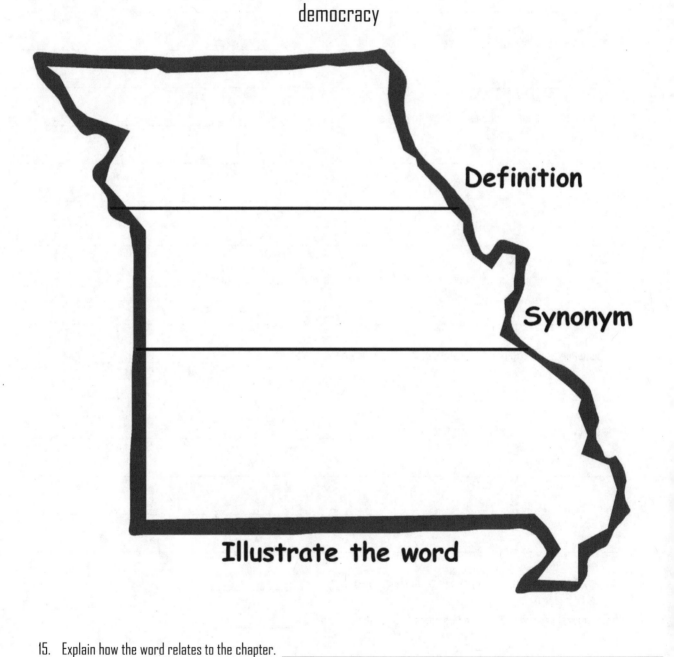

democracy

Definition

Synonym

Illustrate the word

15. Explain how the word relates to the chapter. _____

_____

74   (continued on next page)

Name: _____

CHAPTER 6 ASSESSMENT (cont.)

Demonstrating Your Knowledge

16. Pioneers had a very cooperative spirit. They helped one another with tasks and even had fun while working. Is the spirit of people today still cooperative? Write a paragraph comparing the spirit of the pioneers with the spirit of people in the twenty-first century. Explain your reasoning.

(continued on next page)

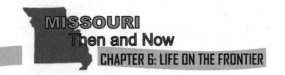
Name: _____

CHAPTER 6 ASSESSMENT (cont.)

17. Look at the picture of pioneers on page 124 of your textbook. How did their lives differ from those of people today? Compare and contrast the life of a pioneer with the life of a person in the twenty-first century. List three points in each column below.

Pioneer Life	Twenty-first-century Life

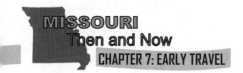

OBJECTIVES

Spaces are provided below each objective for notes taken during reading and class discussions of the chapter and to assist in preparation for the chapter assessment.

In Chapter 7, we will discover and learn about:

The Importance of the Rivers

Flatboats and Keelboats

Steamboats

The Steamboat *Arabia*

OBJECTIVES (cont.)

Early Roads

The Railroad

Samuel Clemens

Riverboat Pilots

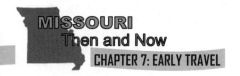

VOCABULARY INSIGHTS

1. dugout

    a. Definition: _____

    _____

    b. Write a sentence from the chapter using the word: _____

    _____

    c. Create your own sentence: _____

    _____

    d. Illustrate the word:

2. keelboat

    a. Definition: _____

    _____

    b. Write a sentence from the chapter using the word: _____

    _____

    c. Create your own sentence: _____

    _____

    d. Illustrate the word:

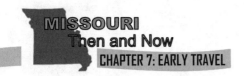

VOCABULARY INSIGHTS (cont.)

3. sandbar

    a. Definition: _____

_____

    b. Write a sentence from the chapter using the word: _____

_____

    c. Create your own sentence: _____

_____

    d. Illustrate the word:

4. steamboat

    a. Definition: _____

_____

    b. Write a sentence from the chapter using the word: _____

_____

    c. Create your own sentence: _____

_____

    d. Illustrate the word:

Then and Now

CHAPTER 7: EARLY TRAVEL

Name: _____

EARLY TRAVEL IN MISSOURI

Outline the history of transportation in Chapter 7 of our text. Write the travel methods above the boxes (omit "early roads") and give details about the methods inside the boxes.

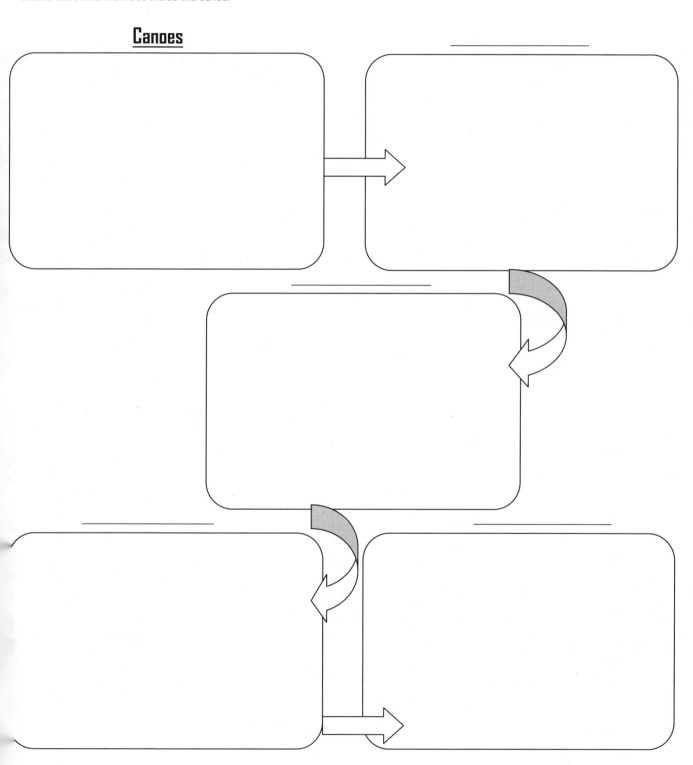

Canoes

Name: _____

RIVER TRAVEL

List the positive and negative aspects of river travel in the boxes below.

Positive Aspects of River Travel	Negative Aspects of River Travel

Name: _____

STEAMBOAT *ARABIA*

Using information from the textbook, your creative writing skills, and the Arabia Steamboat Museum web site, write a detailed account of the sinking of the Arabia from a passenger's point of view.

Arabia Steamboat Museum: http://www.1856.com/story2.html

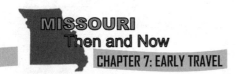
Name: _____

CONTRASTING RIVER TRAVEL

Compare and contrast the different river-travel methods using the graphic organizer.

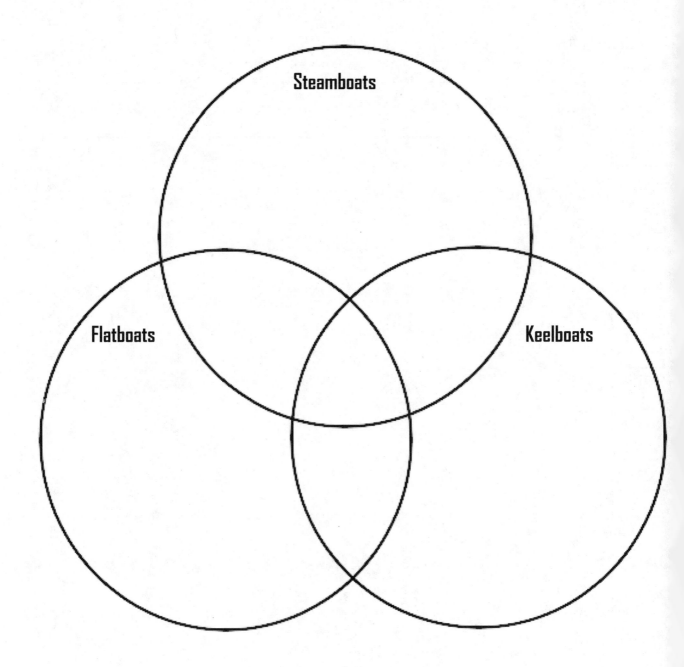

CHAPTER 7: EARLY TRAVEL

Name: _____

CHAPTER 7 ASSESSMENT

Vocabulary

1. Below is a word used in the chapter. In the spaces provided, write a definition of the word, list a synonym for the word, and draw a picture that illustrates the word's meaning.

sandbar

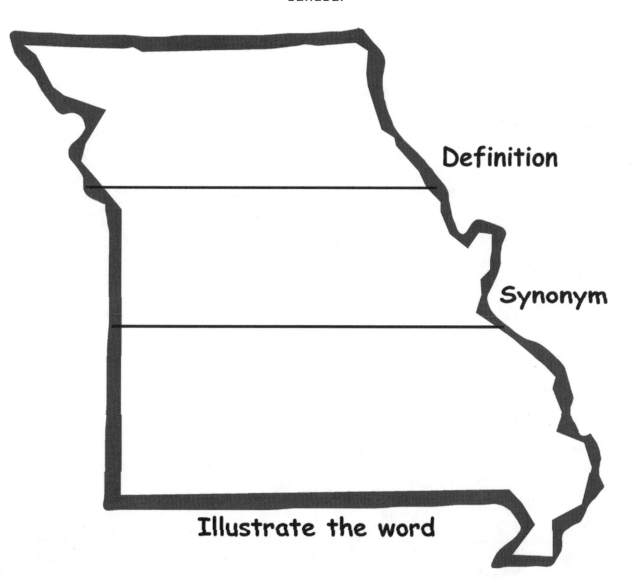

2. Explain how the word relates to the chapter. _____

_____

85

Name: _____

CHAPTER 7 ASSESSMENT (cont.)

Short Answers

3.   Name four kinds of boats that early Missourians used to navigate the rivers. _____,

_____, _____, _____

4.   Early Missouri roads were often built by _____

5.   Pulling a rope tied to a boat's mast as boat crews walked along the bank was called _____.

6.   Missouri's first highways were _____.

7.   A _____ was a one-way craft on the river.

8.   Which famous Missouri writer had previously been a riverboat pilot? _____

9.   What knowledge did a steamboat pilot have to possess to navigate up and down the rivers successfully?

_____

_____

10.   What effect did the building of the railroads have on early Missourians' travel?

_____

_____

11.   What caused the steamboat *Arabia* to sink in the Missouri River? _____

_____

12.   What does the phrase, "By the mark, twain!" mean? _____

_____

13.   Describe Missouri's first roads. _____

_____

_____

(continued on next page)

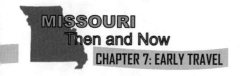

Name: _____

CHAPTER 7 ASSESSMENT (cont.)

True or False

If a statement is false, write the correction on the blank to the right of the statement. (This applies only to statements marked false.)

14. _____ Flatboats were better than keelboats and replaced them on the rivers.

_____

15. _____ When a steamboat came to town, people would gather to watch the boat dock.

_____

16. _____ The pilot had the most important job on a steamboat.

_____

17. _____ The early settlers depended mostly on river travel.

_____

18. _____ Railroads could not operate in many kinds of weather.

_____

19. _____ Early roads were easy to travel on with wagons.

_____

Demonstrating Your Knowledge

20. Discuss four advantages that steamboat transportation brought to the settlers.

(continued on next page)

CHAPTER 7 ASSESSMENT (cont.)

21. Describe why most early Missourians preferred to travel by boat rather than on horseback or by wagon.

22. Beginning with canoes, explain the historical chain of events of early travel in Missouri.

OBJECTIVES

Spaces are provided below each objective for notes taken during reading and class discussions of the chapter and to assist in preparation for the chapter assessment.

In Chapter 8, we will discover and learn about:

The Pony Express

Missouri's Location: The Gateway to the West

Mountain Men

The Oregon Trail

OBJECTIVES (cont.)

The Santa Fe Trail

The California Trail

Key People in the Chapter

The Jumping-Off Place and Western Missouri Cities

90

Name: _____

VOCABULARY INSIGHTS

1. apprentice

    a. Definition: _____

_____

    b. Write a sentence from the chapter using the word: _____

_____

    c. Create your own sentence: _____

_____

    d. Illustrate the word:

2. fortune

    a. Definition: _____

_____

    b. Write a sentence from the chapter using the word: _____

_____

    c. Create your own sentence: _____

_____

    d. Illustrate the word:

VOCABULARY INSIGHTS (cont.)

3. passport

    a. Definition: _____

_____

    b. Write a sentence from the chapter using the word: _____

_____

    c. Create your own sentence: _____

_____

    d. Illustrate the word:

4. stagecoach

    a. Definition: _____

_____

    b. Write a sentence from the chapter using the word: _____

_____

    c. Create your own sentence: _____

_____

    d. Illustrate the word:

Name: _____

PONY EXPRESS RIDER JOURNAL

Write a journal entry of a day in the life of a Pony Express rider carrying mail from St. Joseph, Missouri, to Sacramento, California. Be imaginative. Include obstacles that you encounter, dangerous situations, and details of your trip.

April 15, 1860

MOUNTAIN-MAN CARTOON

Using the blank cartoon panels below, create an exciting mountain-man adventure.

4.	1.

5.	2.

6.	3.

Name: _____

THE TRIP TO SACRAMENTO

How would a trip to Sacramento be different today than it was in 1860? Use the diagram below to compare and contrast.

The Pony Express in 1860   Similarities   The Present

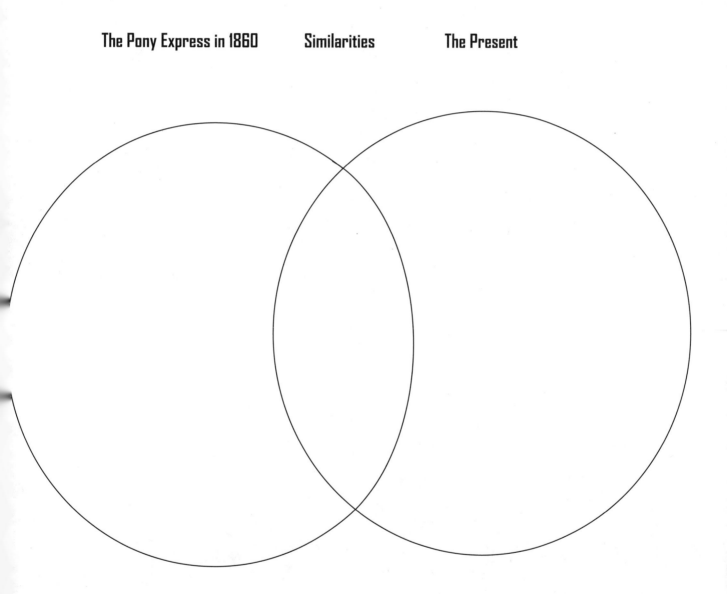

Name: _____

TRAILS WEST

During the move westward by the settlers, Missouri became the "jumping off" place. Create a diagram below comparing the Oregon Trail, the Santa Fe Trail, and the California Trail.

Name: _____

CHAPTER 8 ASSESSMENT

Short Answers

1. Who was considered the "Father of the Santa Fe trade?" _____

2. Which saddlemaker's apprentice ran away to explore Santa Fe? _____

3. Riders for the Pony Express could weigh no more than _____.

4. Stagecoaches carried not only passengers but also _____ from Missouri to the West.

5. Missouri was known as the _____ to the _____.

6. How long did the Pony Express last? _____

7. Mountain men later served as _____ for people traveling west.

8. What caused the Pony Express to go out of business? _____

Who Am I?

9. I was born a slave in Virginia. My family and I moved to Missouri when I was ten years old. When I grew up, I lived and hunted with Crow Indians. I became one of the best trappers and fur traders in the American West. I also worked as a scout for the United States Army. My life was so exciting that I wrote my autobiography, which made me famous.

    Who am I? _____

10. I organized a company to carry mail between Missouri and California. The mail was transported in horse-drawn carriages that also carried passengers.

    Who am I? _____

11. I was a free black businessman with one of the largest businesses in Independence, Missouri. I manufactured wagons and ox yokes. I wasn't always a free man. I was born a slave and made enough money to buy freedom for my wife and myself. The Civil War forced me to leave Independence, and my property was destroyed. I lost most of the money I had made in my business.

    Who am I? _____

Name: _____

CHAPTER 8 ASSESSMENT (cont.)

Vocabulary

12. Below is a word used in the chapter. In the spaces provided, write a definition of the word, list a synonym for the word, and draw a picture that illustrates the word's meaning.

apprentice

13. Explain how the word relates to the chapter. _____

_____

CHAPTER 8 ASSESSMENT (cont.)

True or False

14. _____ Trappers became known as mountain men.

15. _____ The Gateway Arch is located in Ste. Genevieve, Missouri.

16. _____ Charles Orrick was a trader.

17. _____ The Santa Fe Trail made Independence an important jumping-off place for Americans traveling west.

18. _____ Stephen Austin carried out his father's plans to invite Americans to settle in Texas.

Demonstrating Your Knowledge

19. The Pony Express wanted the mail to be delivered by skinny, wiry orphans under the age of eighteen who were expert riders. Use your inference skills to determine why orphans were preferred.

20. Describe how Missouri's location influenced people to migrate to the state and resulted in its becoming the Gateway to the West.

(continued on next page)

Name: _____

CHAPTER 8 ASSESSMENT (cont.)

Comparing Trails

21. Differentiate between the Santa Fe Trail, the Oregon Trail, and the California Trail. Explain why people chose to travel these trails to the West.

Santa Fe Trail	Oregon Trail	California Trail

OBJECTIVES

Spaces are provided below each objective for notes taken during reading and class discussions of the chapter and to assist in preparation for the chapter assessment.

In Chapter 9, we will discover and learn about:

The Differences between the Northern and Southern Settlers

Government and Politics

Immigrants Come to Missouri

The Growth of Towns and Cities

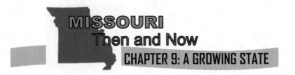

OBJECTIVES (cont.)

Changes on the Farm

Missouri Botanical Garden

German Contributions to Missouri Culture

Manufacturing in Missouri

Name: _____

VOCABULARY INSIGHTS

1. clergyman

    a. Definition: _____

    _____

    b. Write a sentence from the chapter using the word: _____

    _____

    c. Create your own sentence: _____

    _____

    d. Illustrate the word:

2. immigrant

    a. Definition: _____

    _____

    b. Write a sentence from the chapter using the word: _____

    _____

    c. Create your own sentence: _____

    _____

    d. Illustrate the word:

VOCABULARY INSIGHTS (cont.)

3. stollen

    a. Definition: _____

    _____

    b. Write a sentence from the chapter using the word: _____

    _____

    c. Create your own sentence: _____

    _____

    d. Illustrate the word:

4. sauerbraten

    a. Definition: _____

    _____

    b. Write a sentence from the chapter using the word: _____

    _____

    c. Create your own sentence: _____

    _____

    d. Illustrate the word:

Name: _____

NORTH AND SOUTH

Missouri entered the Union as a slave state. Settlers from both northern and southern states came there to live. Some southerners brought their slaves with them. The Yankee settlers did not own slaves or believe in slavery. Suppose a southern slave-owning settler was a neighbor to a Yankee settler. How do you think they got along together? Do you think they sat down and discussed the slavery issue? An important part of life is getting along with others and being able to listen to and understand their point of view. With that in mind, write two paragraphs from the differing points of view of the northern and southern settlers.

First, pretend that you are a Yankee settler in Missouri. Defend your point of view against slavery. Give valid reasons that slavery is wrong.

Now pretend that you are a southern settler in Missouri from a long line of ancestors that were slave owners. Defend your point of view about slavery to your neighbor.

Name: _____

DEMOCRACY THEN AND NOW

List three activities practiced in pre-Civil War Missouri that would be considered undemocratic today.

1.

2.

3.

Write a paragraph to discuss why these activities would be considered undemocratic today.

MISSOURI POLITICIANS

During this exciting time in Missouri's history, several men with ideas about democracy were instrumental in helping the state grow. Three of these men were Andrew Jackson, Thomas Hart Benton, and George Caleb Bingham. After reading Chapter 9, choose which of these men you would like to have been in this time period. Write about this person on the following page. Links are provided below for additional research material.

Andrew Jackson

The Hermitage, Home of President Andrew Jackson: http://www.thehermitage.com/
State Library of North Carolina: http://statelibrary.dcr.state.nc.us/nc/bio/public/jackson.htm

Thomas Hart Benton

Fact Monster: http://www.factmonster.com/ce6/people/A0807071.html
u-s-history.com: http://www.u-s-history.com/pages/h274.html

George Caleb Bingham

Kansas City Public Library: http://www.kclibrary.org/sc/bio/bingham.htm
Fact Monster: http://www.factmonster.com/ce6/people/A0807596.html

Name: _____

MISSOURI POLITICIANS (cont.)

The political person that I would most like to be if I could go back in Missouri's history is:

The reason I have chosen this person is:

The one thing I would change in this person's history is:

CHAPTER 9 ASSESSMENT

Short Answers

1. Which group of people took an active role in electing officials to run the state and the country?

   _____

2. Many early pioneer farms changed into small _____.

3. What continent did most of Missouri's new immigrants come from? _____

4. Which was the largest group of foreign immigrants to come to Missouri? _____

5. Which immigrants were so poor they couldn't buy land and had to settle in the cities?

   _____

6. At first, most manufacturing was done in the _____.

7. The Missouri Botanical Garden was established by _____.

8. Who was called the people's president? _____

True or False

9. _____ Missouri's first elections were held by secret ballot.

10. _____ Andrew Jackson was opposed to democracy.

11. _____ When the Germans came to Missouri, they opposed slavery.

12. _____ Wooden plows replaced iron and steel plows on the growing farms and plantations.

13. _____ The subjects of George Caleb Bingham's paintings were often trappers, boatmen, and voters.

14. _____ By the time of the Civil War, Missouri was no longer a frontier state.

15. _____ Sauerbraten originated in Ireland.

16. _____ The German immigrant Henriette Bruns felt that frontier life in Missouri was easy.

Name: _____

CHAPTER 9 ASSESSMENT (cont.)

Demonstrating Your Knowledge

17. What were the differences between Yankee and southern settlers in Missouri?

18. Characterize the difference between an election in pre–Civil War Missouri and an election today.

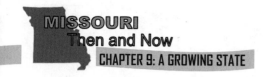

Name: _____

CHAPTER 9 ASSESSMENT (cont.)

19. Describe how the arrival of German immigrants enriched the cultural diversity of Missouri.

20. Explain where the immigrants came from and give four reasons why they came to Missouri.

(continued on next page)

CHAPTER 9 ASSESSMENT (cont.)

Vocabulary

21. Below is a word used in the chapter. In the spaces provided, write a definition of the word, list a synonym for the word, and draw a picture that illustrates the word's meaning.

immigrant

Definition

Synonym

Illustrate the word

22. Explain how the word relates to the chapter. _____

_____

CHAPTER 9 ASSESSMENT (cont.)

Demonstrating Your Knowledge

23. Imagine that you are an immigrant in Missouri in 1837. Describe the hardships and positive aspects of living in this new land.

24. George Caleb Bingham painted pictures of frontier Missouri life and events that had meaning to him, as in his paintings *Order No. Eleven* and *The County Election*. In the box below, draw a picture that you feel represents a growing frontier Missouri.

OBJECTIVES

Spaces are provided below each objective for notes taken during reading and class discussions of the chapter and to assist in preparation for the chapter assessment.

In Chapter 10, we will discover and learn about:

Differences between the North and South

Events Leading to the Civil War

Slave Life

The Debate over Slavery

MISSOURI
Then and Now
CHAPTER 10: A DIVIDED COUNTRY

OBJECTIVES (cont.)

Trouble along the Missouri-Kansas Border

Free African Americans

Key People Leading to the Civil War

Abraham Lincoln

VOCABULARY INSIGHTS

1. abolitionist

a. Definition: _____

_____

b. Write a sentence from the chapter using the word: _____

_____

c. Create your own sentence: _____

_____

d. Illustrate the word:

2. cooper

a. Definition: _____

_____

b. Write a sentence from the chapter using the word: _____

_____

c. Create your own sentence: _____

_____

d. Illustrate the word:

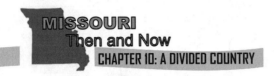

VOCABULARY INSIGHTS (cont.)

3. cabinetmaker

    a. Definition: _____

_____

    b. Write a sentence from the chapter using the word: _____

_____

    c. Create your own sentence: _____

_____

    d. Illustrate the word:

4. Jayhawker

    a. Definition: _____

_____

    b. Write a sentence from the chapter using the word: _____

_____

    c. Create your own sentence: _____

_____

    d. Illustrate the word:

Name: _____

COMPARING FREEDOMS

In the graphic organizer below, compare the lives of slave children to the lives of children today. List everything you know about each subject in the columns provided.

Slave Children's Lives	Children's Lives Today

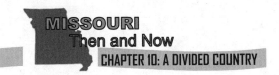

Name: _____

MISSOURI IMMIGRANTS AND SLAVES
Slaves and immigrants both came to Missouri for important reasons. What were they? Compare and contrast these two groups of people that found themselves far away from their homelands.

Slaves	Similarities	Immigrants

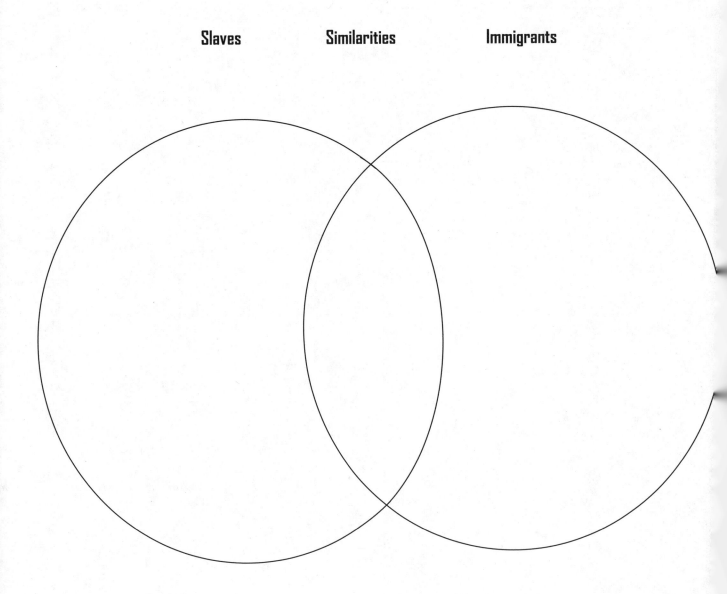

Name: _____

NORTH VS. SOUTH, Part A

In the space below, use a graphic organizer of your choice to demonstrate your knowledge of how the North and South were different.

NORTH VS. SOUTH, Part B

Using the information about the North and South from your graphic organizer, write a paragraph detailing their differences and similarities. Write a rough draft on notebook paper and your final draft in the space below.

Name: _____

JAYHAWKERS: A CLASS DISCUSSION

Jayhawkers did not approve of slavery and felt so strongly that they were known to attack Missourians who believed in slavery and to destroy their property. Some Missourians were just as passionate about their rights to own slaves. In Kansas, some people were even killed in the fighting over slavery, and the state became known as Bleeding Kansas.

Does having differing opinions and strong feelings about an issue give people the right to damage property or hurt others? Write an article about your point of view on this subject.

_____ (Name of Article)

By:

Name: _____

CHAPTER 10 ASSESSMENT

Short Answers

1. Slaves were treated like _____ and not like people.

2. Which slave's court case decision caused a larger division between the North and South over slavery?

   _____

3. Free blacks did not have the same _____ that white people had, but were better off than slaves.

4. Who was president at the time of the Civil War? _____

5. What was the name of the new country formed by the Southern states that seceded from the Union?

   _____

Who Am I?

6. I was a wealthy black businessman in St. Louis. I owned a barrel factory and two steamboats. I started a school for black children in St. Louis so that they could learn to read and write. The officials closed it down because it was against the law. I did not give up, but built a steamboat and turned it into a school. Classes were held in the middle of the Mississippi River and the officials could not do anything about it. My school became known as the freedom school.

   Who am I? _____

7. My wife and I were Missouri slaves who tried to win our freedom in court. We lost our case. Later, a St. Louis businessman bought our freedom. The court decision is one of the most famous in American history.

   Who am I? _____

8. We were Kansans who attacked pro-slavery Missourians and destroyed their property.

   Who are we? _____

9. We were Missourians who crossed over into Kansas to attack antislavery Kansans and burn their homes.

   Who are we? _____

Name: _____

CHAPTER 10 ASSESSMENT (cont.)

Vocabulary

10. Below is a word used in the chapter. In the spaces provided, write a definition of the word, list a synonym for the word, and draw a picture that illustrates the word's meaning.

Jayhawker

Definition

Synonym

Illustrate the word

11. Explain how the word relates to the chapter. _____

_____

Name: _____

CHAPTER 10 ASSESSMENT (cont.)

True or False

12. _____ Most African Americans lived in the Southern states before the Civil War.

13. _____ Slaves could own property and have guns.

14. _____ All African Americans were slaves.

15. _____ Most Southerners voted for Abraham Lincoln for president.

16. _____ The Southern states contained the most people.

17. _____ Some states left the Union after Lincoln was elected president.

18. _____ Slaves worked from sunup to sundown on every day except Sunday.

19. _____ The Dred Scott decision caused the split between the North and South over slavery to grow.

20. _____ Lincoln was a supporter of slavery.

Demonstrating Your Knowledge

21. Explain why you think it was illegal for African Americans to learn to read and write.

(continued on next page)

Name: _____

CHAPTER 10 ASSESSMENT (cont.)

22. Write a paragraph describing the differences between the Northern states and the Southern states.

(continued on next page)

CHAPTER 10 ASSESSMENT (cont.)

Cause and Effect

23. Fill in the cause-and-effect chain of events that led to the Civil War.

THE CAUSE

A debate began between the North and South over slavery.

OBJECTIVES

Spaces are provided below each objective for notes taken during reading and class discussions of the chapter and to assist in preparation for the chapter assessment.

In Chapter 11, we will discover and learn about:

Missouri's Predicament in the War

Border, Confederate, and Union States

The Emancipation Proclamation

Women and African Americans' Role in the Civil War

OBJECTIVES (cont.)

The Results of the Civil War

Order Number 11 and the Guerrillas

Disease and Infections during the War

Germans and African Americans in the Union Movement

Name: _____

VOCABULARY INSIGHTS

1. border

    a. Definition: _____

_____

    b. Write a sentence from the chapter using the word: _____

_____

    c. Create your own sentence: _____

_____

    d. Illustrate the word:

2. guerrillas

    a. Definition: _____

_____

    b. Write a sentence from the chapter using the word: _____

_____

    c. Create your own sentence: _____

_____

    d. Illustrate the word:

VOCABULARY INSIGHTS (cont.)

3. infection

    a. Definition: _____

_____

    b. Write a sentence from the chapter using the word: _____

_____

    c. Create your own sentence: _____

_____

    d. Illustrate the word:

4. retreat

    a. Definition: _____

_____

    b. Write a sentence from the chapter using the word: _____

_____

    c. Create your own sentence: _____

_____

    d. Illustrate the word:

Name: _____

CIVIL WAR MAP

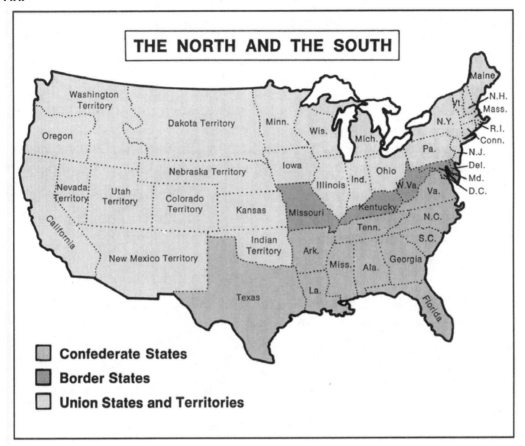

THE NORTH AND THE SOUTH

Washington Territory
Oregon
Dakota Territory
Minn.
Wis.
Mich.
Maine
N.H.
Vt.
Mass.
N.Y.
R.I.
Conn.
Pa.
N.J.
Del.
Md.
D.C.
Nevada Territory
Utah Territory
Colorado Territory
Nebraska Territory
Iowa
Illinois
Ind.
Ohio
W.Va.
Va.
California
Kansas
Missouri
Kentucky
N.C.
Tenn.
S.C.
New Mexico Territory
Indian Territory
Ark.
Miss.
Ala.
Georgia
Texas
La.
Florida

☐ **Confederate States**
■ **Border States**
☐ **Union States and Territories**

1. How many Confederate states were there? _____ List them: _____

    _____

2. Where did Kentucky stand in the Civil War? _____

3. How many border states were there? _____

4. Where did Kansas stand in the Civil War? _____

5. Missouri was a border state. What state is to the south of Missouri, and what kind of state was it?

    _____

6. According to the map, what is a likely reason that Missouri became a battleground during the Civil War?

    _____

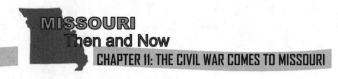

Name: _____

BORDER STATES

The border states were slave states that shared a border with free states to the north. These included Maryland, Kentucky, Virginia, Delaware, and Missouri. Slave states had to make a difficult choice: they had to decide whether to support the North or the South. Missouri became a divided state. Some Missourians wanted to join the Southern states and secede from the Union and others wanted Missouri to remain a part of the United States. Consequently, neighbors fought one another. Sometimes family members fought on opposing sides. The North controlled Missouri during the Civil War. Missouri became a battleground whenever Confederate soldiers tried to take Missouri away from the North.

Can you imagine your homeland becoming a battleground and a civil war taking place in your town? What if your family members were fighting on opposite sides? Illustrate a scene below that portrays the emotions you would feel if this were happening in your community and to you.

Name: _____

WOMEN DURING THE CIVIL WAR

Using the diagram below, compare the roles of frontier women before the Civil War and women during the war.

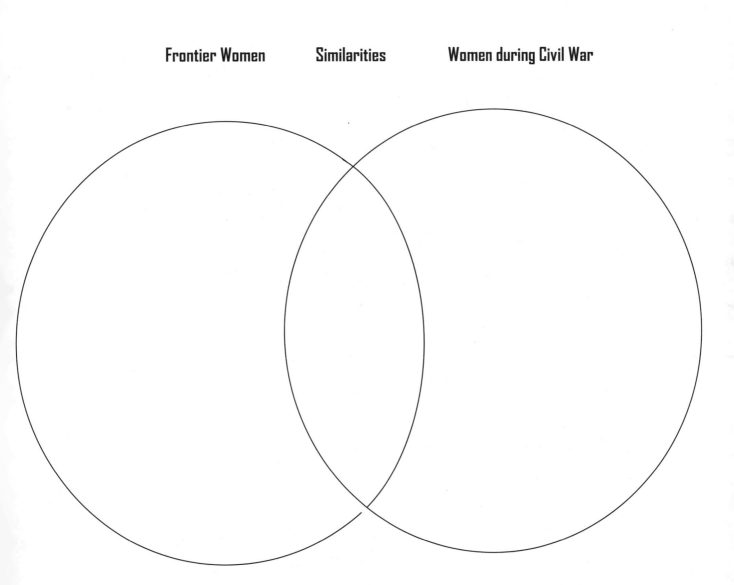

| Frontier Women | Similarities | Women during Civil War |

MISSOURI
Then and Now
CHAPTER 11: THE CIVIL WAR COMES TO MISSOURI

GUERRILLA FIGHTING AND ORDER NUMBER 11

Union troops in Missouri killed and mistreated people whom they believed were helping the Confederate·guerrillas. In the painting on page 223 of your textbook, George Caleb Bingham, the Missouri artist we read about in Chapter 9 of our text, portrayed the results of Order Number Eleven, which forced people in western Missouri to leave their homes. Look carefully at the painting to answer the following questions.

1.   To quote a famous saying, "A picture is worth a thousand words." What do you think this painting is trying to say?

_____

2.   What do you think the young lady in front of the general is saying? _____

_____

3.   Notice the strong use of body language in the painting. What do you think has happened to the man in the foreground who is lying on his back? _____

Why do you think this has happened to him? _____

4.   What do you think are the feelings of the man on the right who is leaving the scene? _____

_____

5.   What is the person on the balcony doing?_____

6.   How would you feel if you were forced to leave your home? _____

Name: _____

PROBLEM SOLVING IN A DEMOCRACY

In Chapter 10, we learned of the Jayhawkers, who felt that slavery was wrong. They felt so strongly that they attacked pro-slavery Missourians and destroyed their property. Later, when Order Number 11 was issued, some people, including the artist George Caleb Bingham, felt strongly about the fact that people were being forced from their homes.

1. How did the Jayhawkers and George Caleb Bingham differ in the ways they showed their strong feelings about issues that were important to them?

2. In an upcoming election, there is an amendment on the ballot that you feel strongly is not in the best interest of your community or state. What can you do to express your feelings and try to initiate change? List four positive and constructive things you can do.

a. _____

b. _____

c. _____

d. _____

CHAPTER 11 ASSESSMENT

Short Answers

1. Explain a positive and negative aspect of Order Number Eleven, which forced people in western Missouri to leave their homes.

   _____

   _____

   _____

2. Why do you think African Americans fought to keep Missouri in the Union?

   _____

   _____

3. Explain why many of Missouri's German people, such as Francis P. Blair, Jr., joined the movement to keep Missouri in the Union.

   _____

   _____

4. Do you think General Sterling Price might have owned slaves? Explain your answer.

   _____

   _____

5. Why did more people in the Civil War die as a result of disease rather than in battle?

   _____

   _____

Name: _____

CHAPTER 11 ASSESSMENT (cont.)

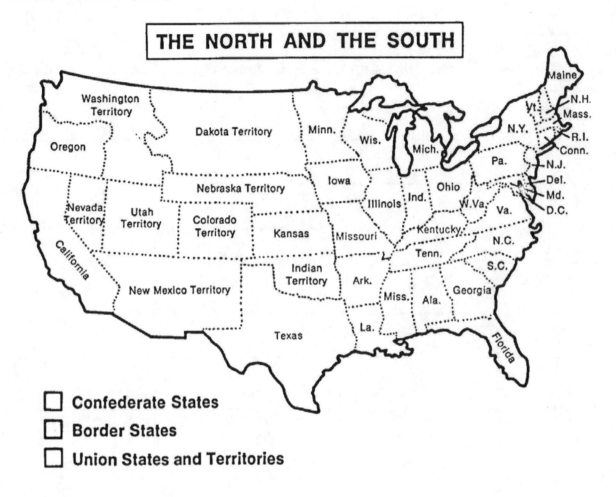

THE NORTH AND THE SOUTH

☐ **Confederate States**
☐ **Border States**
☐ **Union States and Territories**

6. Shade the border states in red and list them. _____

_____

7. Shade the Confederate states in gray.

8. Shade the Union states in blue.

9. What special problems did the state of Missouri have during the Civil War?

_____

_____

142

CHAPTER 11 ASSESSMENT (cont.)

Vocabulary

10. Below is a word used in the chapter. In the spaces provided, write a definition of the word, list a synonym for the word, and draw a picture that illustrates the word's meaning.

guerrillas

Definition

Synonym

Illustrate the word

11. Explain how the word relates to the chapter. _____

_____

Name: _____

CHAPTER 11 ASSESSMENT (cont.)

Demonstrating Your Knowledge

12. What effect did the Emancipation Proclamation have on Missourians and slavery?

13. The Civil War lasted four years and left more than 600,000 Americans dead. List two other results of the war. In your opinion, was the war worth it? Explain.

14. Describe the role that women played during the Civil War and the new opportunities that resulted.

OBJECTIVES

Spaces are provided below each objective for notes taken during reading and class discussions of the chapter and to assist in preparation for the chapter assessment.

In Chapter 12, we will discover and learn about:

Reconstruction and the Emotional and Physical Climate of Missouri after the War

The Right to Vote

Postwar African Americans

Abraham Lincoln

OBJECTIVES (cont.)

The Outlaw State

The Impact of the Railroad

The Radicals

James Milton Turner

Name: _____

VOCABULARY INSIGHTS

1. outlaw

   a. Definition: _____

   _____

   b. Write a sentence from the chapter using the word: _____

   _____

   c. Create your own sentence: _____

   _____

   d. Illustrate the word:

2. bushwhacker

   a. Definition: _____

   _____

   b. Write a sentence from the chapter using the word: _____

   _____

   c. Create your own sentence: _____

   _____

   d. Illustrate the word:

VOCABULARY INSIGHTS (cont.)

3. Reconstruction

a. Definition: _____

_____

b. Write a sentence from the chapter using the word: _____

_____

c. Create your own sentence: _____

_____

d. Illustrate the word:

4. segregated

a. Definition: _____

_____

b. Write a sentence from the chapter using the word: _____

_____

c. Create your own sentence: _____

_____

d. Illustrate the word:

Name: _____

AFRICAN AMERICAN RIGHTS

List the liberties, rights, and freedoms asked for in each box.

Liberties, Rights, and Freedoms African Americans Did Not Have before the Civil War

Liberties, Rights, and Freedoms African Americans Gained after the Civil War

Name: _____

THE OUTLAW STATE

The James gang gave Missouri a bad name by robbing banks and trains. Using information from the chapter, create a wanted poster for Jesse James and the James gang.

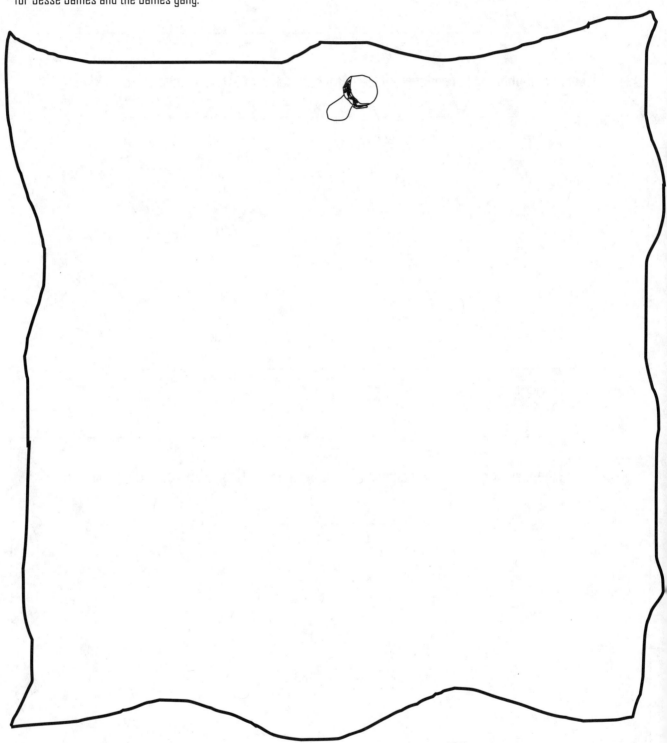

Name: _____

RADICALS AND RECONSTRUCTION

Radical leaders were in charge of Missouri at the end of the Civil War. They passed some harsh laws but also did some good things for Missouri as well. Create a graphic organizer to demonstrate your knowledge of the positive and negative things the Radicals did for Missouri.

Name: _____

RAILROADS AFTER THE CIVIL WAR

As we read in Chapter 7, steamboats brought many changes to Missouri. After the Civil War, railroads became the preferred method of transportation.

Using Chapters 7 and 12 as a reference, brainstorm ideas below as to why the railroads replaced the steamboat as the most important means of transport and way to travel.

Use your ideas above to write a paragraph explaining why railroads replaced the steamboat as the best way to travel and to transport goods.

Name: _____

CHAPTER 12 ASSESSMENT

Short Answers

1. What two groups attempted to gain the right to vote after the Civil War? Did they succeed in their attempt?

_____

_____

2. What was the state of mind of Missourians after the Civil War?

_____

_____

3. What influenced the James gang to become outlaws?

_____

_____

4. Could John Wilkes Booth have been a Radical? Explain.

_____

_____

5. Why is the period after the Civil War called Reconstruction?

_____

_____

(continued on next page)

Name: _____

CHAPTER 12 ASSESSMENT (cont.)

Vocabulary

6.   Below is a word used in the chapter. In the spaces provided, write a definition of the word, list a synonym for the word, and draw a picture that illustrates the word's meaning.

Reconstruction

Definition

Synonym

Illustrate the word

7.   Explain how the word relates to the chapter. _____

_____

Name: _____

CHAPTER 12 ASSESSMENT (cont.)

Demonstrating Your Knowledge

8. Explain the impact of the railroad on Missouri's growth.

9. Describe the positive and negative things the Radicals did for the state of Missouri after the Civil War.

continued on next page)

Name: _____

CHAPTER 12 ASSESSMENT (cont.)

Venn Diagram

10. Compare and contrast the rights of African Americans before and after the Civil War. List at least three differences.

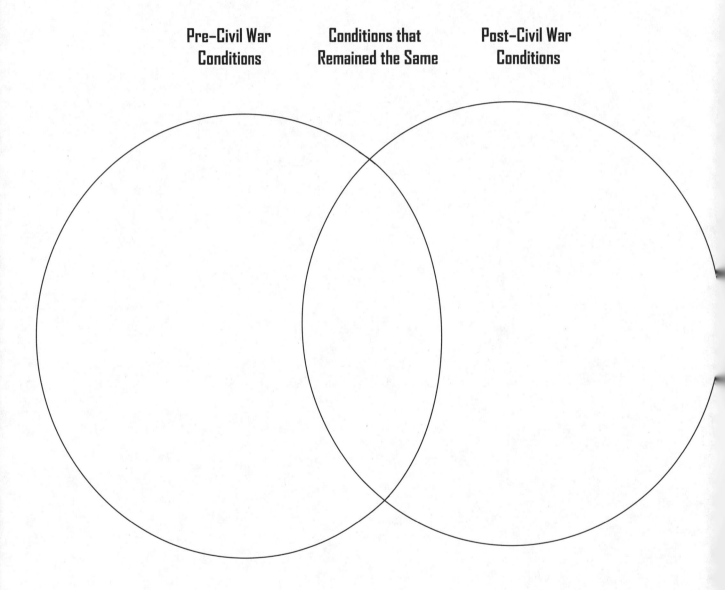

Pre–Civil War
Conditions

Conditions that
Remained the Same

Post–Civil War
Conditions

CHAPTER 13: CHANGING TIMES IN MISSOURI

OBJECTIVES

Spaces are provided below each objective for notes taken during reading and class discussions of the chapter and to assist in preparation for the chapter assessment.

In Chapter 13, we will discover and learn about:

The St. Louis World's Fair

The Impact of Factories on Missouri Life

George Washington Carver

General and Department Stores

OBJECTIVES (cont.)

Machinery in Farming

Women in the Workforce

Inventions

Susan Elizabeth Blow

Name: _____

VOCABULARY INSIGHTS

1. consumer

    a. Definition: _____

    _____

    b. Write a sentence from the chapter using the word: _____

    _____

    c. Create your own sentence: _____

    _____

    d. Illustrate the word:

2. fertilizer

    a. Definition: _____

    _____

    b. Write a sentence from the chapter using the word: _____

    _____

    c. Create your own sentence: _____

    _____

    d. Illustrate the word:

CHAPTER 13: CHANGING TIMES IN MISSOURI

VOCABULARY INSIGHTS (cont.)

3. kerosene

    a. Definition: _____

_____

    b. Write a sentence from the chapter using the word: _____

_____

    c. Create your own sentence: _____

_____

    d. Illustrate the word:

4. licorice

    a. Definition: _____

_____

    b. Write a sentence from the chapter using the word: _____

_____

    c. Create your own sentence: _____

_____

    d. Illustrate the word:

Name: _____

AUTOMOBILES

The first automobiles were very different from the cars of today, as were road conditions. The first cars had to travel on narrow dirt roads and often got stuck in the mud. They could not go very fast. The Missouri General Assembly passed a law to set the speed limit at 9 miles per hour. Determine how long it would have taken you to drive to the St. Louis World's Fair from the following locations.

Starting from:	Miles to St. Louis	Approximate travel time @ 9 mph
Kansas City	234 miles	_____ hours
Hannibal	99 miles	_____ hours
Springfield	198 miles	_____ hours
Poplar Bluff	135 miles	_____ hours
Jefferson City	108 miles	_____ hours
Warrensburg	189 miles	_____ hours
Joplin	252 miles	_____ hours
Smithville	234 miles	_____ hours
Kennett	171 miles	_____ hours
West Plains	153 miles	_____ hours

Name: _____

POSTCARD FROM THE ST. LOUIS WORLD'S FAIR

On the postcard below, write a message to your aunt in Kansas City inviting her to come to St. Louis to join you at the World's Fair. Describe some of the new and exciting things she will see there.

Design the front of your postcard with some of the images you described from the World's Fair.

Name: _____

INVENTIONS

Many new inventions after the Civil War brought changes to the way Missourians lived, worked, and played. Circle one of the inventions below and explain in paragraph form how your life would be different today if it had not been invented.

lightbulb   camera   toilet   hot and cold running water   automobile

vacuum cleaner   electric iron   phonograph   bathtub   telephone

Name: _____

LOUISIANA PURCHASE/WORLD'S FAIR

Read the paragraphs and fill in the blanks using the words in the Word Bank below.

The Louisiana Purchase _____, also known as the 1904 World's Fair, was held to commemorate the 100th anniversary of the Louisiana _____ from the French ruler, _____, by the United States. The purchase of the Louisiana Territory _____ the size of the United States. It included the land that we now know as the states of Arkansas, Oklahoma, Missouri, Kansas, Nebraska, Iowa, North and South Dakota, and Montana, and parts of Minnesota, Wyoming, and Colorado. The Louisiana Territory covered all the land between the _____ River and the Rocky _____. The land deal cost the United States _____ million dollars, which amounted to only a few _____ an acre.

The 1904 World's Fair was a spectacular event that took six years to build. Originally, the fair was due to open a year earlier, but it ran behind schedule and was delayed until 1904. Many new _____ were introduced at the fair. The fairgrounds covered more than twelve hundred _____. More than 12 million people from all over the world came to the fair to celebrate the anniversary of the Louisiana Purchase.

Word Bank:

Mississippi	doubled	Purchase	inventions	cents
Exposition	acres	Napoleon	fifteen	Mountains

164

Name: _____

GROWTH OF MISSOURI CITIES

Many people moved to Missouri cities after the Civil War. Explain why people moved from farms and small towns into large cities and what was responsible for the growth of cities.

In the space below, draw a picture of St. Louis as it may have looked before the Civil War.

In the space below, draw a picture of St. Louis as it may have looked after the Civil War.

Name: _____

WOMEN, THEN AND NOW

Write a paragraph comparing society's expectations of a young girl in 1904 with society's expectations of girls today. Discuss employment, careers, education, and rights. Brainstorm your ideas on a separate sheet of paper and write your final draft below.

Name: _____

GEORGE WASHINGTON CARVER

Read about the life and accomplishments of this famous Missourian at http://www.nps.gov/gwca/expanded/gwc.htm.
Create a story in the boxes below using the most important events in his life.

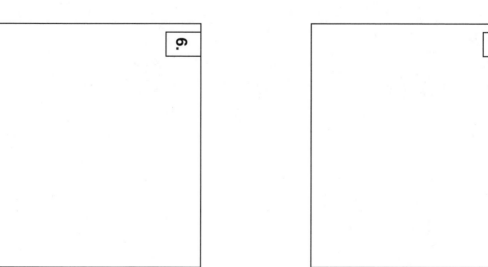

167

Name: _____

CHAPTER 13 ASSESSMENT

Short Answers

1. What impact did George Washington Carver have on Missouri?

    _____

    _____

2. Why did people move into the cities in Missouri in the years after the Civil War?

    _____

    _____

3. The St. Louis World's Fair was held to commemorate the 100th anniversary of what event?

    _____

4. List the different kinds of progress that farmers achieved in Missouri in the years after the Civil War.

    _____

    _____

    _____

(continued on next page)

Name: _____

CHAPTER 13 ASSESSMENT (cont.)

Demonstrating Your Knowledge

5. Summarize the changes in women's roles in society since 1904.

6. Choose three inventions from the chapter and describe the effect they had on Missourians' lives.

(continued on next page)

Name: _____

CHAPTER 13 ASSESSMENT (cont.)

Vocabulary

7. Below is a word used in the chapter. In the spaces provided, write a definition of the word, list a synonym for the word, and draw a picture that illustrates the word's meaning.

consumer

Definition

Synonym

Illustrate the word

8. Explain how the word relates to the chapter. _____

_____

Name: _____

CHAPTER 13 ASSESSMENT (cont.)

Demonstrating Your Knowledge

9. Differentiate between department stores and general stores.

10. List five things a visitor might have seen at the Louisiana Purchase Exposition. Give details.

OBJECTIVES

Spaces are provided below each objective for notes taken during reading and class discussions of the chapter and to assist in preparation for the chapter assessment.

In Chapter 14, we will discover and learn about:

World War I: Allied and Central Powers

Patriotic Missourians

The Roaring Twenties

Charles Lindbergh

OBJECTIVES (cont.)

African Americans and the Quest for Civil Rights

The Great Depression

Changes in Women's Roles

Name: _____

VOCABULARY INSIGHTS

1. commander

    a. Definition: _____

_____

    b. Write a sentence from the chapter using the word: _____

_____

    c. Create your own sentence: _____

_____

    d. Illustrate the word:

2. depression

    a. Definition: _____

_____

    b. Write a sentence from the chapter using the word: _____

_____

    c. Create your own sentence: _____

_____

    d. Illustrate the word:

VOCABULARY INSIGHTS (cont.)

3. submarine

    a. Definition: _____

_____

    b. Write a sentence from the chapter using the word: _____

_____

    c. Create your own sentence: _____

_____

    d. Illustrate the word:

4. victory

    a. Definition: _____

_____

    b. Write a sentence from the chapter using the word: _____

_____

    c. Create your own sentence: _____

_____

    d. Illustrate the word:

BLACK MISSOURIANS AFTER WORLD WAR I

Write a paragraph about the situation of African Americans in Missouri after World War I. Describe the strides that African Americans made to pave the way for others and end segregation in Missouri. You may use the lives of specific African Americans as examples.

Brainstorm your ideas and write a rough draft on notebook paper. Write your final draft below.

Name: _____

COMPARING THE DEPRESSION WITH THE PRESENT

Times were hard during the Great Depression. People had to make things last and be creative to survive. But Missourians are very resilient people.

Explain how Thomas and Lulah May, the couple described in your textbook, provided food, clothing, and toys for their family during the Great Depression.

Food	Clothing	Toys

Describe how your family provides food, clothing, and toys.

Food	Clothing	Toys

Name: _____

VOLUNTEERISM IN MISSOURI

Look carefully at the poster on page 280 of your textbook. What do you think the United States Food Administration was encouraging Missouri citizens to do? What is meant by the slogan, "Food Is Ammunition - Don't Waste It?"

List three ways in which Missourians helped the war effort.

Name: _____

POSTWAR MISSOURI

Compare the progress made in Missouri after the Civil War with the progress made after World War I. What are the similarities? What was the frame of mind of Missourians after these wars? Demonstrate your knowledge in the graphic organizer below.

Post–Civil War Missouri (1865)	Post–World War I Missouri (1920s)	Similarities
Economic Progress	Economic Progress	Economic Progress
Transportation	Transportation	Transportation
Postwar Frame of Mind	Postwar Frame of Mind	Postwar Frame of Mind

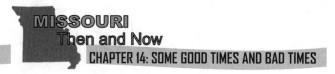
Name: _____

CHAPTER 14 ASSESSMENT

Short Answers

1. Great Britain, France, Russia, and some other smaller nations were on one side during World War I. They were called the _____.

2. When the United States joined in the war, it became one of the _____.

3. World War I lasted from _____ to _____.

4. Which side won World War I? _____

5. The year 1929 was the beginning of hard times in America. What was this period called?

   _____

6. What was the name of Charles Lindbergh's plane? _____

7. Which famous Missourian was called "Captain Harry" during World War I?

   _____

8. Name three new weapons that changed the way World War I was fought.

   _____, _____, and _____.

True or False

9. ____ During the 1930s, white and black baseball players played on the same teams.

10. ____ African Americans and women could vote in the 1930s.

11. ____ Submarines were called U-boats by the Germans.

12. ____ The national government hired people without jobs during the Great Depression.

13. ____ During the depression, the May family bought their meat and mushrooms at the grocery store.

continued on next page)

Name: _____

CHAPTER 14 ASSESSMENT (cont.)

Vocabulary

14. Below is a word used in the chapter. In the spaces provided, write a definition of the word, list a synonym for the word, and draw a picture that illustrates the word's meaning.

depression

Definition

Synonym

Illustrate the word

15. Explain how the word relates to the chapter. _____

_____

Name: _____

CHAPTER 14 ASSESSMENT (cont.)

Demonstrating Your Knowledge

16. How might a child of the Great Depression feel about brand name and designer clothing that children wear today? Explain your reasoning.

17. Describe three ways that Missourians helped the war effort during World War I. Are these things that Missourians would do today to help during a war?

    a)

    b)

    c)

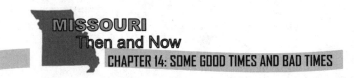
Name: _____

CHAPTER 14 ASSESSMENT (cont.)

18.   Create a graphic organizer to illustrate the status of African Americans' fight for equal rights between the wars.

OBJECTIVES

Spaces are provided below each objective for notes taken during reading and class discussions of the chapter and to assist in preparation for the chapter assessment.

In Chapter 15, we will discover and learn about:

World War II: The Cause

Axis and Allied Powers

Pearl Harbor, Hawaii

Missouri Military Leaders

CHAPTER 15 OBJECTIVES (cont.)

Patriotic Missourians and the War Effort

Harry S. Truman

Civil Rights Movement

The Women's Movement

Name: _____

VOCABULARY INSIGHTS

1. dictator

   a. Definition: _____

   _____

   b. Write a sentence from the chapter using the word: _____

   _____

   c. Create your own sentence: _____

   _____

   d. Illustrate the word:

2. barracks

   a. Definition: _____

   _____

   b. Write a sentence from the chapter using the word: _____

   _____

   c. Create your own sentence: _____

   _____

   d. Illustrate the word:

CHAPTER 15: MISSOURIANS JOIN STRUGGLES

VOCABULARY INSIGHTS (cont.)

3. peace

    a. Definition: _____

    _____

    b. Write a sentence from the chapter using the word: _____

    _____

    c. Create your own sentence: _____

    _____

    d. Illustrate the word:

4. recycle

    a. Definition: _____

    _____

    b. Write a sentence from the chapter using the word: _____

    _____

    c. Create your own sentence: _____

    _____

    d. Illustrate the word:

Name: _____

HOW WORLD WAR II BEGAN

Fill in the chart to show the chain of events that led the U.S. to declare war on the Axis Powers.

THE BEGINNING

The United States Congress declares war on Japan and the other Axis countries.

Name: _____

PATRIOTIC MISSOURIANS

Just as they did in World War I, Missourians stepped up and did their part to help in the war effort during World War II. Create a graphic organizer below to compare and contrast the ways in which Missourians helped the war effort during the two world wars.

Name: _____

TIMELINE

Choose five events from Chapter 15 and create a timeline. Write an appropriate title for your timeline in the box provided below.

Name: _____

ORDINARY CITIZENS

Ordinary people can accomplish great things. Some examples are Ivory Perry, Captain Wendell Pruitt, and Lucile H. Bluford. Think about your school or neighborhood. Are there conditions or problems that you would like to change to make your world a better place? How can you go about creating change in a positive way? Identify a problem and a plan of action, and illustrate them in the circle below.

Problem:

Plan of Action:

CHAPTER 15 ASSESSMENT

Vocabulary

1. Below is a word used in the chapter. In the spaces provided, write a definition of the word, list a synonym for the word, and draw a picture that illustrates the word's meaning.

dictator

Definition

Synonym

Illustrate the word

2. Explain how the word relates to the chapter. _____

_____

Name: _____

CHAPTER 15 ASSESSMENT (cont.)

Short Answers

3. List four characteristics that made Harry S. Truman a remarkable man and a great president.

    _____

    _____

4. Which of the two powers fighting in World War II did not believe in democracy? Give an example of this side's undemocratic behavior.

    _____

    _____

5. The United States did not want to get involved in World War II. What was the last straw that forced the country to declare war?

    _____

    _____

6. What circumstances caused Truman to become president?

    _____

    _____

7. Explain the reason for the Civil Rights movement.

    _____

    _____

Name: _____

CHAPTER 15 ASSESSMENT (cont.)

Using Inference Skills

8. The United States was founded on the concept of democracy, yet African Americans and women fought for equal rights for many decades. Why do you think it took so long for these two groups to attain equal rights?

9. Several people in this chapter worked to improve humankind and made the world a better place through their efforts. Think about the lives of these people and, in paragraph form, describe the qualities you believe ordinary people must possess in order to be able to make positive changes in the world.

(continued on next page)

Name: _____

CHAPTER 15 ASSESSMENT (cont.)

10. Missourians are patriotic and loyal people. Compare and contrast the ways they helped their country through two wars.

COMPARING MISSOURIANS' WAR EFFORTS

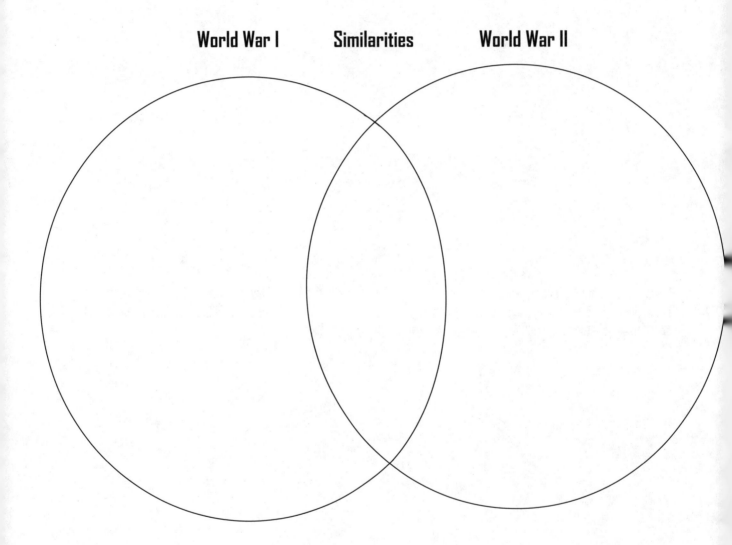

World War I   Similarities   World War II

OBJECTIVES

Spaces are provided below each objective for notes taken during reading and class discussions of the chapter and to assist in preparation for the chapter assessment.

In Chapter 16, we will discover and learn about:

Rules and Laws

Democracy

Services Provided by the U.S. Government

State Government

OBJECTIVES (cont.)

National Government

City Government

County Government

Taxes

Name: _____

CHAPTER 16: GOVERNMENT IN MISSOURI

VOCABULARY INSIGHTS

1. county

    a. Definition: _____

    _____

    b. Write a sentence from the chapter using the word: _____

    _____

    c. Create your own sentence: _____

    _____

    d. Illustrate the word:

2. income tax

    a. Definition: _____

    _____

    b. Write a sentence from the chapter using the words: _____

    _____

    c. Create your own sentence: _____

    _____

    d. Illustrate the words:

VOCABULARY INSIGHTS (cont.)

3. jury

    a. Definition: _____

_____

    b. Write a sentence from the chapter using the word: _____

_____

    c. Create your own sentence: _____

_____

    d. Illustrate the word:

4. mayor

    a. Definition: _____

_____

    b. Write a sentence from the chapter using the word: _____

_____

    c. Create your own sentence: _____

_____

    d. Illustrate the word:

Name: _____

STATE GOVERNMENT

Label the Missouri government chart correctly and explain the job of each branch.

```
              ┌─────────────────────────┐
              │    Missouri Government  │
              │     (State Government)  │
              └─────────────────────────┘
                          │
      ┌───────────────────┼───────────────────┐
    (     )             (     )             (     )
      │                   │                   │
  ┌───────┐           ┌───────┐           ┌───────┐
  │       │           │       │           │       │
  │       │           │       │           │       │
  └───────┘           └───────┘           └───────┘
```

Name: _____

NATIONAL GOVERNMENT

Label the U.S. government chart correctly and explain the job of each branch.

United States Government
(National Government)

Name: _____

COMPARING STATE AND NATIONAL GOVERNMENTS

Use the diagram below to compare and contrast the state government and national government.

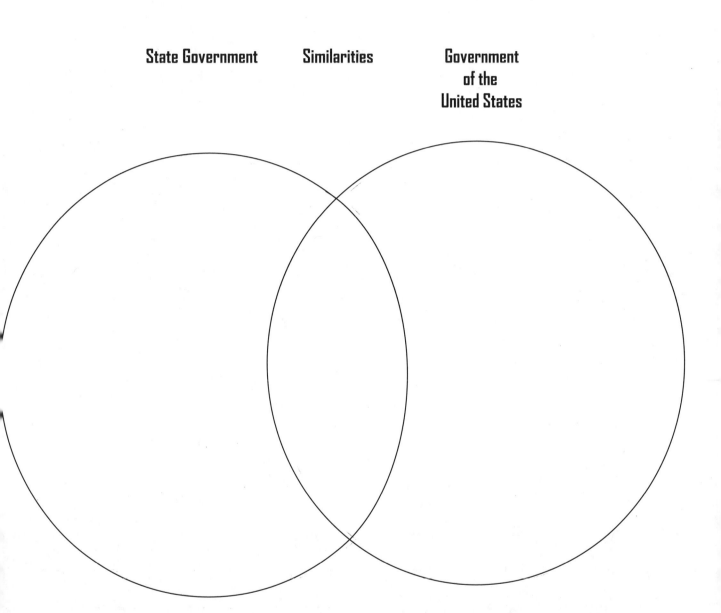

State Government   Similarities   Government
of the
United States

Name: _____

THE IMPORTANCE OF LAWS

Governments were set up to make laws and to make sure that everyone follows them. Laws are like rules. Can you imagine what our society would be like without laws to protect us?

On the left side of the chart, list four laws that we have to follow as citizens. On the right, explain what would happen if we didn't have those laws.

Four laws:	Consequences of not having laws:
	 _____ _____ _____
	 _____ _____ _____
	 _____ _____ _____
	 _____ _____ _____

Name: _____

RESPONSIBILITIES OF GOOD CITIZENS

A democracy is a government run by the people. Citizens of a democracy have certain responsibilities. In the boxes below, list the five main responsibilities that citizens must assume in order for democracy to work well.

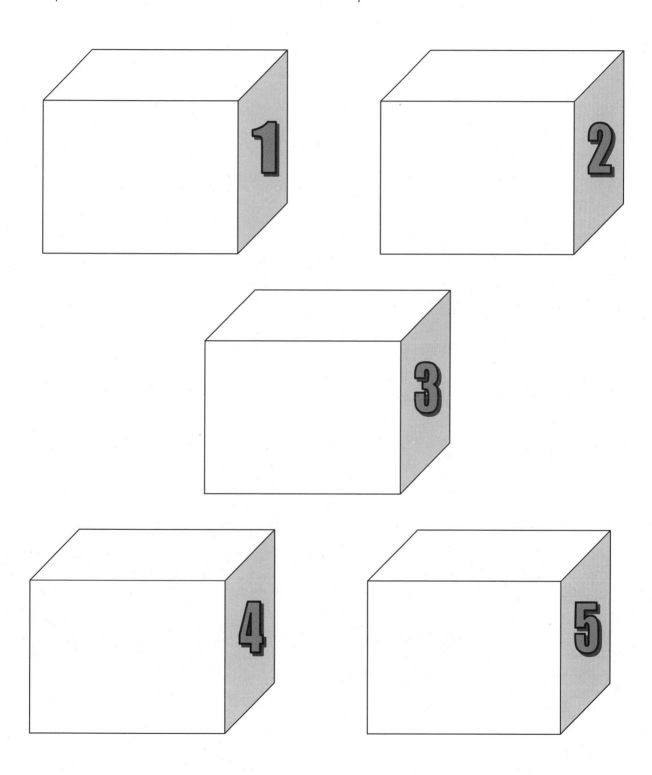

Name: _____

CHAPTER 16 ASSESSMENT

True or False

1. _____ The president makes the laws.

2. _____ The government gets money from the people.

3. _____ The General Assembly makes laws for the state.

4. _____ The Bill of Rights protects our freedom of speech.

5. _____ The Supreme Court is in the legislative branch.

6. _____ Today some countries are run by dictators.

7. _____ In a democracy, people elect their leaders.

8. _____ Citizens of a democracy have responsibilities.

9. _____ The mayor is the leader of the county.

10. _____ The sheriff works for the city.

Short Answers

11. What type of tax is added to the price of things you buy? _____

12. What type of tax is based on the money you earn? _____

13. What type of tax provides schools, libraries, cities, and counties with money? _____

14. The group of people who run a city is the _____.

15. Why do we have governments? _____

_____

_____

(continued on next page)

Name: _____

CHAPTER 16 ASSESSMENT (cont.)

16. What are the three branches of the state government? _____

_____

17. Why do the people of a democratic government elect leaders? _____

_____

Demonstrating Your Knowledge

18. a) Explain why laws or rules are important.
    b) Create a rule that would be valuable to your classroom or school, and explain why it is needed.

19. a) Explain the term *democracy* and the responsibilities of citizens in a democracy.
    b) Name one responsibility you have as a member of your classroom, and explain why it is important.

(continued on next page)

CHAPTER 16 ASSESSMENT (cont.)

20. Explain how the government gets money in order to run our country.

(continued on next page)

Name: _____

CHAPTER 16 ASSESSMENT (cont.)

Vocabulary

21. Below is a word used in the chapter. In the spaces provided, write a definition of the word, list a synonym for the word, and draw a picture that illustrates the word's meaning.

jury

Definition

Synonym

Illustrate the word

22. Explain how the word relates to the chapter. _____

_____

CHAPTER 16 ASSESSMENT (cont.)

23. Draw a diagram comparing the state and national governments. Describe each branch, its responsibilities, and its leader.

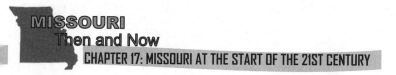
OBJECTIVES

Spaces are provided below each objective for notes taken during reading and class discussions of the chapter and to assist in preparation for the chapter assessment.

In Chapter 17, we will discover and learn about:

The Information Age

Computers in Farming and Manufacturing

Providing Services and Products

Selling Goods: Sam Walton and J. C. Penney

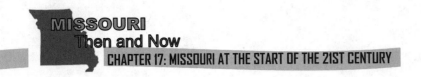
OBJECTIVES (cont.)

The Tourist Industry

The Importance of the Mississippi and Missouri Rivers

Missouri Conservation

Transportation

VOCABULARY INSIGHTS

1. erosion

a. Definition: _____

_____

b. Write a sentence from the chapter using the word: _____

_____

c. Create your own sentence: _____

_____

d. Illustrate the word:

2. manufacturing

a. Definition: _____

_____

b. Write a sentence from the chapter using the word: _____

_____

c. Create your own sentence: _____

_____

d. Illustrate the word:

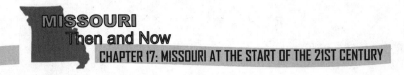

VOCABULARY INSIGHTS (cont.)

3. interstate

a. Definition: _____

_____

b. Write a sentence from the chapter using the word: _____

_____

c. Create your own sentence: _____

_____

d. Illustrate the word:

4. tourist

a. Definition: _____

_____

b. Write a sentence from the chapter using the word: _____

_____

c. Create your own sentence: _____

_____

d. Illustrate the word:

Name: _____

MISSOURI'S FARMING HISTORY

Why do farmers today produce more food than previous generations of farmers? _____

_____

In the spaces below, list the different ways that each group of Missourians farmed the land.

Pioneer Farmers	_____ _____ _____ _____ _____ _____
Post-Civil War Farmers	_____ _____ _____ _____ _____
21ˢᵗ Century Farmers	_____ _____ _____ _____ _____

Name: _____

MISSOURI TRANSPORTATION

Missourians have always been on the move. Through the years they have continued to improve upon methods of transportation.

1. How many methods of transportation can you recall from Missouri's history? Write them down and state which one you think has had the biggest impact on Missourians.

2. Write a paragraph about why you think the method of transportation you chose was the one that made the biggest impact. Explain your reasoning and identify the information you used to make your decision.

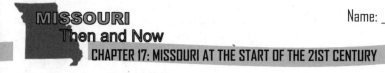

Name: _____

TECHNOLOGY IN MISSOURI

List six different ways that you use technology daily.

1. _____   4. _____

2. _____   5. _____

3. _____   6. _____

How has the invention of the computer affected our lives? Brainstorm your ideas and write a paragraph below explaining how computers have affected the lives of Missourians.

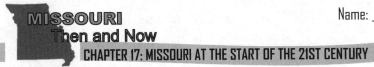

SHOW-ME BROCHURE

Using the template below or a sheet of white paper folded into thirds, research a location in Missouri and design a brochure that will encourage people to visit. Compile some facts and use your creativity to help promote the location.

Name: _____

CHAPTER 17 ASSESSMENT

Vocabulary

1. Below is a word used in the chapter. In the spaces provided, write a definition of the word, list a synonym for the word, and draw a picture that illustrates the word's meaning.

tourist

Definition

Synonym

Illustrate the word

2. Explain how the word relates to the chapter. _____

_____

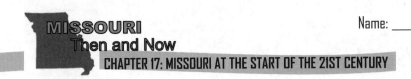

Name: _____

CHAPTER 17 ASSESSMENT (cont.)

Short Answers

3. Missouri has always been a rich land, and many people over the years have enjoyed the state's natural resources. What could happen to our natural resources if they are not protected?

    _____

    _____

4. What was the purpose of the first computers, and when were they built?

    _____

    _____

5. Why is this called the information age?

    _____

    _____

6. Why is more food grown and more products manufactured today despite the fact that there are fewer farmers and factory workers?

    _____

    _____

(continued on next page)

CHAPTER 17 ASSESSMENT (cont.)

Using Inference Skills

7. Explain the difference between providing a service and providing a product. Give an example of each.

8. Missourians Sam Walton and J. C. Penney discovered profitable ways to sell products and became successful businessmen. Explain some things that you would do as a businessperson to increase your business and to bring customers to your products.

9. Missouri has many tourist attractions. Explain how the tourist industry maintains its status as big business and helps Missouri grow.

(continued on next page)

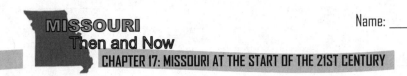
Name: _____

CHAPTER 17 ASSESSMENT (cont.)

10. The Mississippi and Missouri Rivers have always been important to Missourians. Explain the history of the rivers' importance, concluding with their importance today. You may include diagrams or illustrations in your response.

OBJECTIVES

Spaces are provided below each objective for notes taken during reading and class discussions of the chapter and to assist in preparation for the chapter assessment.

In Chapter 18, we will discover and learn about:

Fiction and Ballads

Samuel Clemens

Langston Hughes

Laura Ingalls Wilder

OBJECTIVES (cont.)

Thomas Hart Benton and George Caleb Bingham

Walt Disney

Scott Joplin

The Blues, Ragtime, and Jazz

Name: _____

VOCABULARY INSIGHTS

1. composer

    a. Definition: _____

_____

    b. Write a sentence from the chapter using the word: _____

_____

    c. Create your own sentence: _____

_____

    d. Illustrate the word:

2. cartoon

    a. Definition: _____

_____

    b. Write a sentence from the chapter using the word: _____

_____

    c. Create your own sentence: _____

_____

    d. Illustrate the word:

VOCABULARY INSIGHTS (cont.)

3. mural

    a. Definition: _____

    _____

    b. Write a sentence from the chapter using the word: _____

    _____

    c. Create your own sentence: _____

    _____

    d. Illustrate the word:

4. musician

    a. Definition: _____

    _____

    b. Write a sentence from the chapter using the word: _____

    _____

    c. Create your own sentence: _____

    _____

    d. Illustrate the word:

Name: _____

THOMAS HART BENTON

Thomas Hart Benton, the great-nephew of the Missouri senator of the same name, was a Missouri artist who specialized in painting murals. Much like George Caleb Bingham, he painted things that were happening around him. On page 362 of your textbook is a small part of a mural he painted in the state capitol building.

1. Do you think that artists can express emotion or feeling in a piece of art? Explain.

2. Think about something that is important to you—a person, a problem, or issue that you feel strongly about. Draw a picture to illustrate those feelings. Use expression and body language in your illustration to get your idea across.

Name: _____

LANGSTON HUGHES

Before answering the questions below, read Langston Hughes's poem "Dreams," on page 371 of your textbook.

1. What do you think Hughes meant when he wrote: "Life is a broken-winged bird / That cannot fly"?

    _____

    _____

2. "Hold fast to dreams" means _____.

3. What frame of mind do you think Hughes was in when he wrote the lines "For when dreams go / Life is a barren field / Frozen with snow"?

    _____

4. Do you think the author had any experience with broken or lost dreams? Explain your answer.

    _____

    _____

5. Do you think that dreams were important to the author? Why or why not?

    _____

    _____

Name: _____

COMPARING MISSOURI AUTHORS

Samuel L. Clemens, Langston Hughes, and Laura Ingalls Wilder were all Missouri authors. How did their writing differ? What types of writing did they do? What parts of the state were they from? Answer these questions about each author below.

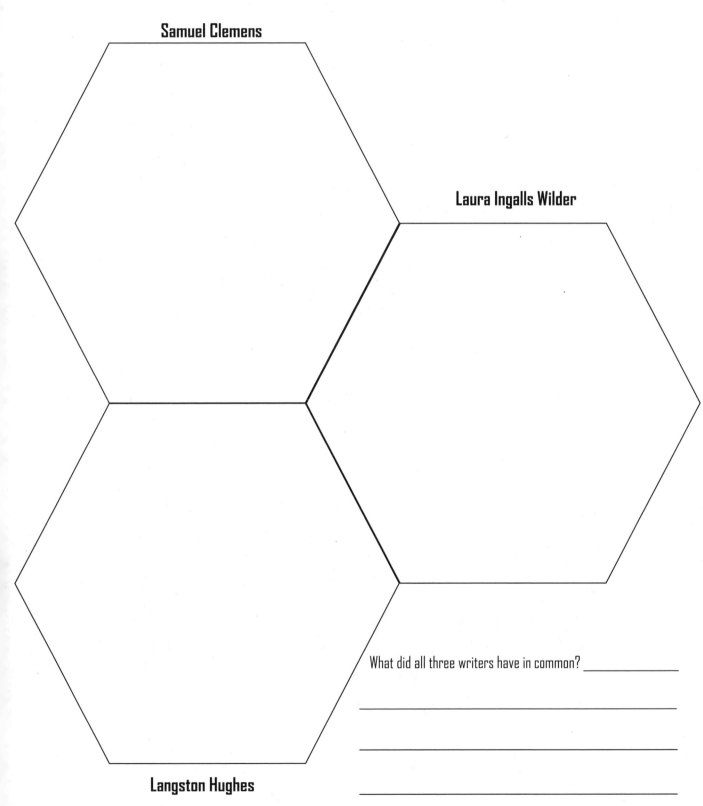

Samuel Clemens

Laura Ingalls Wilder

Langston Hughes

What did all three writers have in common? _____

_____

_____

_____

Name: _____

FICTIONAL STORY

Fiction is writing about things that did not really happen. Authors often write fiction based on familiar things and places. Samuel Clemens was one example. Use your imagination and write a fictional short story based on a familiar place, person, activity, or thing.

Name: _____

WALT DISNEY

Walt Disney was a famous cartoonist and animator. His best-known character was Mickey Mouse. Disney always had faith in his ability to draw. Many people think that they do not have this ability. Let's try a little drawing experiment.

On page 364 of your textbook there is a picture of Mickey Mouse. Turn the picture upside down and draw your own upside-down Mickey in the space below. Begin at the top (with Mickey's feet) and just draw **exactly** what you see, line by line. Do not pay attention to anything else but each line. When you are finished, turn both pictures right-side up, and see how closely your drawing of Mickey matches the original.

Did drawing the picture upside down help? Explain why or why not.

Name: _____

CHAPTER 18 ASSESSMENT

Short Answers

1. Define the term *fiction.* _____

   _____

2. Define the term *ballad.* _____

   _____

3. Who was the "King of Ragtime"? _____

4. Who wrote *Little House on the Prairie*? _____

5. Who created Donald Duck? _____

6. Which artist painted a mural depicting the westward expansion at the Truman Library in Independence, Missouri?

   _____

7. Which Missouri-born author wrote about the African American's struggle to gain respect and honor?

   _____

True or False

8. _____ Eugene Field wrote poems for children.

9. _____ Laura Ingalls Wilder never lived in Missouri.

10. _____ Blues, ragtime, and jazz are types of music that are important to Missouri history.

11. _____ The father of the blues was Langston Hughes.

12. _____ Walt Disney's first full-length movie was *Cinderella.*

13. _____ Fiction is the kind of writing that is always true.

14. _____ Samuel Clemens and Langston Hughes both wrote about the things they knew best.

Name: _____

CHAPTER 18 ASSESSMENT (cont.)

Vocabulary

15. Below is a word used in the chapter. In the spaces provided, write a definition of the word, list a synonym for the word, and draw a picture that illustrates the word's meaning.

mural

Definition

Synonym

Illustrate the word

16. Explain how the word relates to the chapter. _____

_____

Name: _____

CHAPTER 18 ASSESSMENT (cont.)

Using Your Inferencing Skills

17. Though they were born in different time periods, Thomas Hart Benton and George Caleb Bingham were both important Missouri artists. Describe the similarities of their work.

18. Why do you think many writers write about things and events that are familiar to them?

19. Of all the creative Missourians discussed in this chapter, which one do you admire the most? Explain why.

(continued on next page)

Name: _____

CHAPTER 18 ASSESSMENT (cont.)

20. Choose one of the following activities to complete below:
   - Write a poem about the struggles of being a student.
   - Write a fiction story about a school adventure.
   - Write a paragraph about everyday life in Missouri and draw an illustration based on your paragraph.

MISSOURI
Then and Now

WEB SITE BIBLIOGRAPHY

Arabia Steamboat Museum: <http://www.1856.com/index.html>

Thomas Hart Benton. Fact Monster: <http://www.factmonster.com/ce6/people/A0807071.html>

Thomas Hart Benton. U-S-History.com: <http://u-s-history.com/pages/h274.html>

George Caleb Bingham. Kansas City Public Library: <http://kclibrary.org/sc/bio/bingham.htm>

George Caleb Bingham. Fact Monster: <http://www.factmonster.com/ce6/people/A0807596.html>

Nathan Boone Homestead State Historic Site. Missouri State Parks and Historic Sites:
    http://www.mostateparks.com/boonehome/photos.htm>

Boone's Lick State Historic Site. Missouri State Parks and Historic Sites:
    <http://www.mostateparks.com/booneslick/geninfo.htm>

George Washington Carver National Monument. National Park Service: <http://www.nps.gov/gwca/expanded/gwc.htm>

The Hermitage, Home of President Andrew Jackson: <http://www.thehermitage.com>

Andrew Jackson. State Library of North Carolina: <http://statelibrary.dcr.state.nc.us/nc/bio/public/jackson.htm>

Thomas Jefferson's First Inaugural Address. Bartleby: <http://www.bartleby.com/124/pres16.html>

Missouri Constitution. Missouri General Assembly: <http://www.moga.state.mo.us/const/moconstn.htm>

Sainte Genevieve, Mo., Historic Homes. <http://www.saintegenevieve.tourism.org/homes.htm>

Taum Sauk Mountain State Park. Missouri State Parks and Historic Sites:
    <http://www.mostateparks.com/taumsauk/geninfo.htm>